Nonverbal Learning Disabilities

A Guide to School Success

(Middle/High School)

Nonverbal Learning Disabilities

A Guide to School Success

(Middle/High School)

Dean J.M. Mooney, Ph.D., NCSP
Sherry Sousa Newberry, M.A.
Nina Kurtz, M.A.

Nonverbal Learning Disabilities: A Guide to School Success (Middle/High School)
Written by Dr. Dean J.M. Mooney, Sherry Sousa Newberry, and Nina Kurtz

Copyright © 2006 Maple Leaf Center, Inc.
167 North Main Street
Wallingford, VT 05773 USA

Published and Distributed by

Maple Leaf Center
167 North Main Street
Wallingford, VT 05773
Phone (802) 446-3601

Printed in the United States of America

ISBN: 978-0-9759850-2-1
0-9759850-2-7
Library of Congress Control Number: 2006925148

Table of Contents

Preface

Nonverbal Learning Disability is a term used to describe a specific learning profile. It is characterized by a number of cognitive strengths and challenges that impacts a child's success in the academic and social settings. While this colors all aspects of the student's life, it does not limit who he or she can become.

The authors of this book believe that it is important to understand each learner for not *all* students with NLD will have *all* attributes of this disability or fit a specific mold. Every student is unique and each journey through the educational system needs to be determined both from sound educational data and the student's own interests, goals and passions.

The goal of *Nonverbal Learning Disabilities: A Guide to School Success (Middle/High School)* is to share the experiences of three professionals who work with students with NLD in a variety of settings. Working in the roles of teacher, administrator, and clinical/school psychologist, they have taken the time to listen and learn from their students. Whether it is how to best present a writing assignment or how to ask a classmate to a dance, the authors have come to appreciate these students as creative, informed and personable. Each of these students is a strength to the academic setting and peer group.

Rather than focusing on the limitations of this disability, these authors believe that with a quality comprehensive evaluation, a well-informed team, appropriate approaches, and the input of the student, academic and social success can be reached. The authors are excited to share the lessons that they have learned from their students and know that these lessons will assist you in working with students to meet their academic and personal potential.

CHAPTER I

The View from the Brain

What is NLD?

A Nonverbal Learning Disability (NLD) is a neurodevelopmental disorder first defined by Myklebust (1975) as a social perception disability, and then more extensively researched by Rourke et al (1973, 1981, 1985, 1987-1993, 1995-1996, 2000). It typically impacts three areas of functioning including visual spatial/organizational (the ability to interpret and organize the individual's visual-spatial environment), motoric (the ability to master their physical environment and express themselves in written form), and social (the ability to adapt to new or novel situations, and/or accurately read and respond appropriately to nonverbal signals and cues), and is hypothesized to involve the white matter of the brain (including the right hemisphere and the corpus callosum). Nonverbal learning disorders appear much less frequently than language-based learning disorders. NLD is found in approximated 10% of the learning disabled population (approximately 1% of the normal population) and affects females and males equally.

What are the Strengths and Challenges of a Student with NLD

Neuropsychologists typically speak in terms of assets and challenges. For the purpose of this book, we will speak in terms of strengths and challenges. The student with NLD is frequently described as being "smart" by both parents and teachers. In the early grades, many children with NLD display high achievement in subjects that require high memorization but little abstract or conceptual thought. Their perceived intelligence works for them, but also against them by creating an illusion of competence. As a result, their perceived intelligence is their greatest strength, but also one of their worst enemies. These individuals are very aware of their limitations and will often buy into their own illusion of competence, setting higher expectations for themselves in all areas of functioning. Both parents and other adults often experience children with NLD as being more competent than they truly are. Society places a high regard on individuals with good verbal skills, one of the strengths of an individual with NLD. However, this is an overestimation. As a result, many parents and teachers feel that they are being manipulated by this individual when in fact they are not. Parents and teachers frequently ask what behaviors are NLD and what behaviors are typical of normal development. Given that NLD is a syndrome, not all of the strengths and/or challenges identified by Rourke et al. (1989) will be evident in individuals with NLD. In fact, some individuals with NLD display splinter skills or strengths and/or challenges that do not entirely fit the pattern of NLD. For example a student with NLD may show all other strengths and challenges of NLD except for math. Listed below are the strengths and challenges typically found in individuals with NLD by Rourke. This section will also explain how each of these shows itself in the high school environment.

Strengths

Rote Material

Working with repetitive and unchanging information (e.g., saying the capitals of the states, memorizing multiplication tables, reading a script in a play, saying the Pledge of Allegiance, singing the National Anthem) is a strength for the student with NLD. Routine situations are comforting (e.g., Attendance from 9:00

am – 9:10 am, Calendar from 9:10 am – 9:30 am, Library from 9:30 am – 10:00 am, and so on). Students learn that they can rely on these routines and their predictability and gain comfort from them.

Auditory Perception

Students with NLD often have a heightened ability to perceive auditory information. This is the ability to correctly receive information aurally. Students may hear absolutely everything going on around them and may experience this as intrusive. Earlier on in their life, they may have experienced it as oversensitivity to sounds—loud ones in isolation like a concert or more generalized sound like a crowd. They may not yet have learned how to modulate incoming auditory information and could become overwhelmed by a noisy classroom, lunchroom, hallway, or bus.

Auditory Attention

As a result of intact auditory perception, individuals with NLD are more likely to have good auditory attention. This refers to the ability to listen to *sounds* for an extended period of time without tiring or becoming distracted (e.g., listening to music for a long period of time, listening to white noise—the sound of a fan, clothes dryer, running water, a blow dryer). Many students use these techniques to calm themselves and to decompress following a rather stressful day at school. At school, they may need to use these techniques during times of heightened stress (e.g., examinations, presentations).

Auditory Memory

When one is able and willing to attend to auditory information, the likelihood of well rehearsed memory increases—a strength for individuals with NLD. Auditory memory involves the ability to recall and compare auditory information previously heard. This can include words in isolation as well as differences in rhythm patterns, sounds and songs.

Verbal Attention

While similar to the above, this is the ability to listen to the spoken word for extended periods of time without tiring or becoming distracted (e.g., listening to lectures, radio talk shows, or books on tape for long periods of time). This is extremely useful in high school since many faculty rely on a lecture format. What we must keep in mind is that many students with NLD often appear as if they are not listening because they are not using the typical measure of attention—eye contact. This often translates into their not relying on visual input and being diagnosed with Attention Deficit Hyperactivity Disorder—Inattentive Type. This diagnosis should be scrutinized when given to a student with NLD. Use of continuous performance tests that involve visual input, such as the Connors Continuous Performance Test (Multi-Health Systems Incorporated; 2000, 2004), should be avoided at all costs.

Verbal Memory

Students with NLD often display an uncanny ability to recall previously presented verbal information. If this strength is present, they are able to remember word-for-word what was said, including the tone. This often puts these students in great stead with their teachers who can always call on them to answer a question provided the information was presented verbally. Many teachers report that students with NLD appear to memorize everything that they say (e.g., remembering a conversation that was heard, being able to 'parrot' lines from Monty Python movies or other favorite movies.

Other Verbal Strengths

Other verbal strengths include: phonology, verbal reception, verbal repetition, verbal storage, verbal associations and verbal output. These are best understood to educators as 'speech and language' strengths (e.g., talking, verbally interacting with others, having conversations). In early childhood, students with NLD are precociously verbal, often using full sentences while non-NLD peers are still gesturing with single word requests. Early on, peers often look up to these individuals as being fountains of information from which they can drink heartily. Interactions with adults are positively reinforcing because adults are often intrigued by their conversational skills and apparent level of knowledge. As a result they are often deemed gifted by parents or teachers because of society's reliance on verbal production.

Simple Motor Skills

While working on activities requiring simple motor skills (e.g., walking, stacking books), these students do not stand out. Activities that involve simple physical movements with little planning, minimal balance, and minimal hand-eye coordination are seen as a strength for individuals with NLD. However, as with all of the strengths and challenges found in children with NLD, it should be remembered that the more complex the situation becomes, the more demands are placed on a child, and the greater the chance for failure or reduction in competency.

Graphomotor

Graphomotor skills refer to students' abilities to express themselves in written form, through pictures or words, by using their hands, not a keyboard. This has nothing to do with the organization of thoughts or ideas, but strictly with the mechanics of printing, writing, and/or drawing. Earlier research (Rourke,

1989) suggests this is a strength that is developed in the latter grades; however, this has not proven to be the case. Many schools do not employ a consistent and reliable method of teaching printing and writing (e.g., the old Palmer Method) that relies on the over-teaching of skills. As a result, many students with NLD continue to struggle with graphomotor expression late into their educational careers.

Academic Strengths (Decoding, Spelling, Reading)

As a result of the many of the above strengths, students with NLD typically display exceptional decoding and encoding skills (i.e., single word reading,' spelling skills, and reading). Word decoding is simply reading single words in isolation, not in context. Spelling is also known by educators as encoding. This strength involves simply spelling words correctly. Early on in their education, students with NLD are often held up to peers as exemplary readers and spellers. These strengths remain throughout high school. They also display a heightened ability to apply rules of language (e.g., when a word ends in 'y', drop the 'y' and add 'ies' to make it plural). This does not necessarily transfer to a second language; in fact, many students with NLD need an exemption from the second language graduation requirements found in many high schools.

So far, a picture has been painted of a student who appears competent, is probably getting straight A's, and is often relied on by the teacher to answer questions when other students cannot. One would think this to be a picture of a happy and thriving student, certainly a student that every teacher would want to have in his or her classroom. Correct? Not necessarily. As you will soon see, the combination of their strengths, with their challenges, create a very different picture in the classroom.

Challenges

The following are the challenges typically found in students with NLD:

Novel Material

A student's struggle with novel material will reveal itself in his or her desire/need to keep everything as it is in the school and classroom setting. Changes to routine and spontaneity will result in an immediate negative response, usually involving a heightened level of anxiety. The impact of this challenge cannot be underestimated and will be more intensely discussed below under Psychosocial and Adaptive Challenges.

Tactile Perception

The skin is the largest sensory organ available to receive information. Challenges in this area will have a dramatic impact on development throughout a student's school career. To a neurotypical child, spending the day in a primary classroom seems like a dream come true. Bright colors decorate the room, objects hang from the ceiling, the block center is in one corner, the water/sand table is in another, the different textures of beads, beans or noodles are explored in one area of the room, and of course the dress-up corner is in yet another area. What these typical children enjoy about the classroom can be repulsive for the young student with NLD. This later translates into problems involving the ability to hold onto writing instruments with the correct grip and strength without exhausting the hand muscles. While the primary strength of simple motor skills is often found in these students, their tactile perceptual challenges influence their willingness and desire to interact with their environment in a tactile manner (i.e., with their hands). Teachers may see heightened tactile defensiveness and/or heightened tactile sensitivities. It is not only the changes in tactile perception that are uncomfortable, but also the individual sensations themselves that they may react to negatively. Since teens tend to enjoy their own smell (they are always around it so it becomes routine), body odor becomes a problem in adolescence. Another consideration is that the soap, deodorant, or shampoo/ conditioner might not feel good or may have a smell that they cannot tolerate. Season changes or geographic moves can impact tactile sensitivity. For instance, in some geographic regions winter may be a problem in that one's skin may become drier than usual and therefore more sensitive. This obviously impacts social success.

Tactile Attention

Given a history of inaccurate tactile perception, it is understandable that the student with NLD does not pay attention to that which cannot be trusted. Tactile attention is seen in the student's ability to focus on information provided through the skin, primarily as measured through the hands, for an extended period of time without tiring or becoming distracted (e.g., holding a pen, modeling with clay, working with the hands).

Complex Psychomotor Skills

This challenge involves activities that require complex physical movements as well as planning, balance, and/or hand-eye coordination (e.g., riding a bicycle, writing, drawing, dancing, acting out the motions/gestures of a song). Despite their increased verbal abilities, students with NLD struggle to express themselves in written form. In drawing, their visual perception combines with problems of psychomotor expression in rather immature drawings. Handwriting and printing may be slow, laborious, and even unreadable, often even to themselves. This is an area of frustration for these students that remains with them throughout their academic careers. Psychologists need to avoid interpreting their drawings in a projective manner.

Complex Graphomotor Coordination

This refers to the ability to express thoughts or ideas in written form, through pictures or words, by using the hands, not a keyboard. This can include the organization of those thoughts or ideas (e.g., organizing paragraphs, writing a story, reading comprehension, performing mechanical arithmetic, doing mathematics, working with science).

Visual Perception

This primary challenge involves the ability to receive information correctly through the eyes (e.g., to see material on a chalkboard correctly, to see a teacher correctly, to see anything as it truly appears). Visually, students with NLD cannot always make sense of what they perceive. As a result, they may scan the environment furiously in an attempt to try to find visual stimuli that will coincide with what they are hearing. As these students discover that the visual input (i.e., what they are looking at) may conflict with what they hear, they learn to rely less on what they see and more on what they hear. Sometimes they become so overwhelmed by the discrepancy that they attempt to eliminate or ignore visual information. For these students, seeing is not believing. This student may close their eyes, or put their head down on their desk in an attempt to tune in more to their auditory strength. Any changes in school visual environment may set them off. In high school this challenge is seen in subjects such as geography (map reading), math (especially geometry), and the sciences. They may also have difficulty finding their way around school to find the cafeteria, bathroom, or gym. These students frequently get lost in larger schools. The reader is again reminded that as situations become more complex for the student and the student is exposed to more information simultaneously, the greater is the chance of their becoming overwhelmed.

Visual Attention

Since students with NLD cannot trust what they see, they are reluctant to attend to it. Visual attention involves the ability to focus on information provided to us through our eyes for an extended period of time without tiring or becoming distracted (e.g., watching a movie, watching a teacher demonstrate an activity, watching a hockey game). Visual perceptual difficulties and the resulting confusion is often reflected in poor visual attention. Behaviorally, these students may scan the classroom, often appearing to not pay visual attention (eye contact) to the speaker and/or the learning materials (chalkboard, charts). This may be interpreted by teachers as inattention and may even be diagnosed as ADHD-Inattentive Type; however, they are anything but inattentive, they are actually hyper-attentive or hyper-vigilant.

Visual Memory

As a result of the primary and secondary challenges related to vision (Attention and Memory) found in students with NLD, visual memory is often a significant challenge. Students with NLD will struggle to find things in their backpack, lunch bag, desk, classroom and school. As well, just because they found what they were looking for on one occasion, does not guarantee they will find it on another. Visual memory involves the ability to recall and compare information previously seen (e.g., recognizing that you have driven down this road before, recognizing faces of people you have met previously, finding your way back to your classroom).

Exploratory Behavior

All of the primary challenges found in students with NLD (tactile perception, visual perception, complex psychomotor skills and novel material) result in the NLD students' reluctance and/ or inability to adequately explore their environment. Exploratory behavior involves the desire and the willingness to investigate the environment around one's self, (e.g., going for a walk, trying a new food, smelling an unknown flower, seeking out new life and new civilizations and boldly going where no person has gone before—apologies to Gene Roddenberry!). The resulting lack of exploratory behavior has significant impact on their learning. Most people learn through a combination of rote instruction and their experiences in the environment. By removing their environmental experiences, the student with NLD is left with relying strictly on direct instruction of rote material. In each novel situation we have the opportunity to learn something through exploration (e.g., the children who learn all about stingrays at the petting tank on the field trip to the aquarium). A student with NLD will avoid this situation. Instead he or she will opt to read, to the point of memorization, the information plaque. The end result of this field trip is that the typical student has learned by reading the plaque, and also by anchoring that information through the experience with the living stingray through it's feel, movement, sight, shape, and smell. By not participating in the petting tank, the student with NLD has lost the opportunity to reinforce the learning experience through another sense, and has also more than likely missed out on the chance of interacting with aquarium personnel, an opportunity for further social learning. As mentioned previously, the greater and more complex the demands for exploratory behavior, the greater the chance that the challenge (heightened reluctance/refusal) will surface.

Activity Level

A student with NLD typically displays a heightened reluctance to move around his or her environment. This attitude is quite understandable given all of the above mentioned challenges. This most typically involves participation in extra-curricular activities outside of the usual day-to-day routine (e.g., a hike with friends, a dance class, karate, gymnastics, a horseback ride). Most students with NLD exhibit a diminished desire to be active given their history of numerous failures at activities (e.g., soccer, baseball, and other team sports that require appropriate tactile perception, visual planning and attention, complex psycho-motor skills and a working understanding of subjects such as physics, geometry, etc.). As the student with NLD grows older there is a growing reluctance to participate in the day-to-day activities of the school. Given the ongoing lack of social success, there is a strong wish to withdraw from the environment, both at school and at home. If left un-checked, the student will create a cocoon, for protection, by withdrawing to the point of isolation. A reduced level of physical activity and increased passivity is frequently seen in students with NLD. They don't move because they have learned that they are not good at moving around their world—both physically and socially.

Verbal Challenges

Verbal challenges include: oral-motor praxis, prosody, semantics, content, pragmatics, and function. While the speech of a student with NLD appears competent and well developed, further investigation will reveal a lack of understanding of deeper meaning (e.g., idioms, sarcasm, humor). This is one of the larger contributors to some of the obvious social challenges. These verbal challenges also involve how individuals speak (e.g., having inflections in your voice as opposed to using a monotone, robotic-like voice) and understanding others when they use unique language (e.g., idioms—"up a creek without a paddle", verbal humor, morals contained without stories vs. a concrete/ basic understanding of language).

Time sense

A good sense of time involves estimating time and planning accordingly (e.g., being able to judge the time of day, how long it takes to walk to school). This is usually extremely poor in students with NLD. As a result, students may either under or over estimate the time needed to complete tasks. They may show up late or early for classes. On examinations or in testing situations, they display an inability to pace themselves in order to complete all questions.

Psychosocial and Adaptational Challenges

Of all of the areas of challenge, these are the most crucial to be aware of and to accommodate, especially in the school setting. These challenges hinder daily functioning in all areas, not just academic.

Adaptations in Novel Situations

Adaptations in novel situations involves being able to appropriately react to change and adapt one's thoughts or behaviors based on changes to the surrounding environment (e.g., putting a coat on when it suddenly gets cold, reacting appropriately to a substitute teacher or surprise quiz). Students with NLD will react in a highly negative and resistant manner to any changes in situations (i.e., from routine programs all the way down to the small matters in the classroom). Novelty can mean new situations but also adaptations to existing situations (e.g., changing the 9:00 am spelling test to 10:00 am one day). Again, as stated earlier, as the complexity of the novelty increases, so decreases the ability to adjust.

Social Competence

The ability to make and keep friends through appropriate social interactions shows social competence. As the reader will learn, a student with NLD has significant challenges in several areas of social competence. If left un-checked, challenges in social competence are guaranteed to lead to significant psychosocial disturbances. The reader is strongly encouraged to investigate appropriate and timely interventions.

Psychosocial Disturbance

Psychosocial disturbance is best understood as atypical thoughts, feelings and reactions in relation to typical day-to-day stressors (e.g., anxiety, depression, obsessions, compulsions). Virtually all psychosocial disturbance experienced by students with NLD is related to environmental issues. The fewer interventions put in place to support these individuals, the greater the level of psychosocial disturbance. A more in depth discussion and serious discussion of this issue can be found later in this book.

Academic Challenges

Students will typically display challenges in all of the areas listed below. Specific accommodations need to be put in place for these specific subjects as well as other subjects that may contain aspects of these subjects (e.g., mathematics used in home economics, etc.). Further suggested accommodations will be presented later in this work.

Reading Comprehension

Reading comprehension involves understanding the meaning of what has been read at a deeper level, not just parroting what was read (e.g., being able to put a story that you read into your own words).

Mechanical Arithmetic

Students with NLD struggle with being able to complete addition, subtraction, division, and multiplication tasks while maintaining adequate columns and rows (e.g., keeping the one's in the one's column, the ten's in the ten's column and so on).

Of greatest importance when looking as a student's strengths and challenges is the fact that it is the interaction between both the strengths and the challenges that creates the difficulties typically seen in the student with NLD.

TABLE 1

The summary of the neuropsychological strengths and challenges *typically* found in individuals with NLD and how each strength and challenge makes itself apparent in the school environment.

Function	Strength or Challenge	Examples
Activity Level	Challenge	• extracurricular activities • hiking • sports • horseback riding • dance lessons
Adaptations in Novel Situations	Challenge	• reacting to change • disliking spontaneity • struggling with change to routine
Auditory Attention	Strength	• listening to music • listening to lectures • listening to white noise
Auditory Memory	Strength	• remembering what was said • parroting another person
Auditory Perception	Strength	• hearing sounds and words correctly
Complex Graphomotor	Challenge (early)	• writing a story • organizing paragraphs
Complex Psychomotor Skills	Challenge	• riding a bicycle • dancing • gymnastics

Function	Strength or Challenge	Examples
Concept Formation	Challenge	• learning about fairness • learning about friendships • learning about sharing
Emotional Stability	Challenge	• anxiety • depression • obsessions • compulsions • anger • fear • high suicide potential
Exploratory Behavior	Challenge	• taking risks • trying new foods • traveling • going for a walk
Graphomotor	Challenge (early) Strength (late)	• printing • writing • drawing • copying
Mechanical Arithmetic	Challenge	• adding in columns • 'carrying' and 'borrowing'
Novel Material	Challenge	• field trips • spontaneity • schedule changes • new school • anything new
Problem Solving	Challenge	• deductive and inductive reasoning
Reading Comprehension	Challenge	• putting a story in your own words • understanding themes • understanding morals in the story
Rote Material	Strength	• saying the alphabet • counting numbers • saying the "Pledge"

Function	Strength or Challenge	Examples
Rote Material *(continued)*		• memorizing multiplication tables • memorizing a script
Simple Motor Skills	Strength	• walking • clapping hands • stuffing envelopes • stacking blocks
Social Competence	Challenge	• making and keeping friends • appropriate social interactions
Spelling	Strength	• encoding • spelling single words correctly
Tactile Attention	Challenge	For an extended period of time: • playing with toys • playing with clay • working in a tactile center
Tactile Memory	Challenge	• recalling shapes through feel
Tactile Perception	Challenge	• identifying shapes by touch • identifying objects by touch
Time Sense	Challenge	• judging and estimating time
Verbal Attention	Strength	• listening to lectures • listening to talk radio • listening to books on tape
Verbal Memory	Strength	• remember what someone said

Function	Strength or Challenge	Examples
Verbal Memory *(continued)*		• remembering a conversation
VERBAL Oral-Motor Praxis, Prosody, Phonology Semantics, Content, Pragmatics, Function	Challenge	• inflection/emotion in voice • idioms • verbal humor • deeper meaning of language
VERBAL Phonology, Verbal Reception, Verbal Repetition, Verbal Storage, Verbal Associations, Verbal Output	Strength	• talking • interacting verbally with others • having conversations (one-sided)
Verbatim Memory	Strength	• parroting exact conversations • memorizing lines from a movie • memorizing lists of facts
Visual Attention	Challenge	• watching a movie • watching a demonstration • watching a sporting event
Visual Memory	Challenge	• recognizing faces of people • recognizing facial expressions • finding your way around a school
Visual Perception	Challenge	• seeing a chalkboard accurately • following gestures • following hand signals
Word Decoding	Strength	• reading single words in isolation

CHAPTER 2

Students' Perspectives of Nonverbal Learning Disabilities

What Students Have to Say About NLD

Students with Nonverbal Learning Disabilities (NLD) were extremely interesting as well as challenging to interview. Some students were open and had a good understanding of their challenges. Other students were resistant and often avoided answering direct questions. All students interviewed were quite concrete and literal in their varied responses. Many needed revisions of questions to "get the idea".

These students want to go to school events and hang out with friends! This is a familiar statement for any high school student, however, for these adolescents there are few friends to hang out with, and mom and dad have become their social friends. One female student said, " I had a big group of friends that understood my problems in elementary school and middle school, but now they don't have time for me. I feel bad, but I am done with them. They aren't very nice." An adult male student now attending college stated, "I have a couple of buddies that I met after I went to college. We are together after school and on the weekends—the two of them are my best friends. They help me with school a lot." Developing appropriate peer relationships is a dilemma for most adolescent students. The perceptual challenges of students with NLD further complicate this social need.

Navigating Through School

A high school student reported that school takes so much energy: "I have help in the morning at home getting ready. I can't always get my hair just right, and I want to be sure everything is okay. Clothes that I think match are switched by my sister. She is great and helps me a lot. I have medication to take, and I worry I can't do it by myself. I get frustrated and sometimes yell because I just think I can't do it! I know I should be able to do it but it gets jumbled up! School can be so hard. I worry about if I will find my classes, what will my teachers be like, will they understand I am different? What about homework? I have lied about homework because I didn't understand what I was supposed to do. It really helps when someone shows me around school. Sometimes my mom does that, or a friend, or a teacher. There have been times when I just couldn't remember where a room was, and I didn't go to class because I couldn't find the class. I need someone to take me around before school starts and show me where my classes are and how the building is laid out. Once I get it, I get it! It just takes me a whole lot longer to get it!"

The student with NLD is preoccupied by many concerns. These worries range from locating a classroom to interacting with their teachers. While most adolescents have fears regarding the school environment, students who have NLD have the added challenge of rarely feeling at ease at school. Is this the day everyone will find out I am different? As teachers and parents it is encumbent upon us to understand both the role of educators and the world of the student. One without the other minimizes our effectiveness. We may know the neurological implications of NLD, but without the entire program/effort the knowledge is lost.

A middle school student relates his interpretation of all the challenges of middle school: " I was told I had a Nonverbal Learning Disability in Middle School. I knew that school was getting harder, and I was having more difficulty with homework and understanding what was being expected of me. My parents spent a lot of time helping me, and I remember many times going home and not having any idea of what I had for homework. It made for some hard times with my parents. I think they thought I was not paying attention or didn't care. In reality, I just didn't know. My special educator really helped me and made me feel I had someone who understood what I was going through. She was able to help my parents understand and then they were able to help me more. The family disagreements settled down."

Academics

Students report that math and science are the most painful. Research projects are also challenging. Math, particularly geometry, is next to impossible. Understanding spatial relationships and seeing the planes makes this concept incomprehensible. In writing, it is knowing what to write, how much to write, and when to stop. A high school student reported how proud he was of a paper he had written that was over fifty pages long and covered every area of the concept in depth. The assignment was to "state your opinion of the reading." The reading was only one page long. The "state your opinion" part of the assignment was misunderstood. Homework completion is consistently problematic across the board for the student with NLD. Individualized Educational Plan (IEP) teams often discuss whether these students should be held to the same homework standard as other students because of the energy they require to get through a day at school. Some students see themselves as not different and insist on doing all the work, but this comes at the expense of their family support network. These students need incredible support to complete their academics.

Concerns of the Student with NLD

In an almost ramble of consciousness a student reports the following feelings: "I worry about how I am doing, what do people think, what do I have to do. Some of the time I don't even know what I have to do. I go to my special educator who really helps me sort it out. I also go to counseling and that helps me see what I can do and what I can't do. I try to keep it all together, and I find that after a period of time it all swims in my head and I have to get help." Realizing that accessing adult and peer resources is one way to manage individual anxieties is an important first step for students with NLD. This can be an easier concept for some students to understand.

The student in high school is more likely to report the opposite stating, "nothing is wrong." The high school student also will not participate in a social skills support group because he or she doesn't see a need. After a year of few friends and amazing support at home, the student is doing well academically, but the social piece is falling apart. Difficult times within the family are experienced daily with angry outbursts and frustrations. There is depression regarding friends, school, and anything else complicated. The family reports their extreme concern over the isolation that is beginning to occur. They are offering support in all ways, but that doesn't replace friends.

Friends/Peer Relationships

Friends are the driving force behind the social structure of any school. Friends are typically identified for their loyalty, sincerity, common interests, social beliefs, and personality traits. These are all characteristics that can be described and incorporated into an individual. The students with NLD who were interviewed had a difficult time identifying descriptors to the questions regarding friends. Some regarded teachers as friends because of the assistance or personality in the classroom. Friends were more often people they had not known for a long period of time. Their naivete and lack of social evaluation was evident in almost all cases. There was no concern or understanding that friends shouldn't make fun or tease others with disabilities in a detrimental way or acknowledge their friend's disability as weird or annoying. Most interesting was the factual way NLD students categorized friends: that friend is in band, or science, or on the football team.

When asked if they socialize with their friends, older students replied, "Usually one or two." One high school senior shared having a standing outing on Friday afternoon. Nothing could interfere with that date. Parents reported there were many times when the friend didn't show and the student was left with disappointment. The student explained that it was okay, even if he didn't get a call why his friend didn't come. Repeatedly parents reported that they assisted in encouraging, organizing and assisting their child's plan for social activities. It appeared that after high school most students broke away from parental involvement which is developmentally later than their age peers. When asked about sharing interests and conversations with friends, it was clearly a one to two word response. There appeared to be no awareness of the social conventions and conversations that are often evident in a truly rich friendship. The question, "So what do you and your friends talk about?" was too open ended and had to be reframed to specifics.

Clearly the friend issue has to be taught and re-taught. Social scripting and real experience in conversations need to be reviewed many times. Typically, students with NLD struggle with reading facial expressions and body language. They miss much, trying to understand the complexities of our society. Is it a blessing that sometimes these students don't know the big picture. How hurtful are their friends? How hurtful are adults in their lives? Some were able to verbalize their loneliness. They discussed their depression and low self esteem and how school made them feel. So many have gifts in specific areas, and they do find rewards and recognition in these areas.

The primary theme that came from talking with students is the tremendous need to teach them how to survive in the world. Part of their education has to be survival. Their challenges are not going to go away. They do not outgrow NLD; however, they are able to identify environments which are not as socially demanding as the school setting and where their cognitive strengths can allow them to succeed.

CHAPTER 3

Parents' Perspectives of Nonverbal Learning Disabilities

Parents' Views of NLD

Parents share how they have walked and will continue walking through the very complicated and challenging world of NLD with their children and adult children. Parents are very sincere with their thoughts and comments, questions, joys, and pains in responding to their experiences with their children. Parents appreciate the opportunity to learn how to help their children by working with professionals who are knowledgeable in NLD.

"I am so relieved to know this is what it is!" "I knew something was wrong—I just didn't know how or what to do." "I guess my drill sergeant schedule was the right thing to do all along." "We spent thirteen years knowing things were not exactly the way they should be—we regret not knowing sooner." "It all makes sense to us now." These statements represent parents who have and are working diligently to assist their children navigate their NLD world effectively.

Challenges of Parenting these Children

Most say that parenting these children is "lonely, difficult, and exhausting." It is lonely, because no one but parents can begin to understand how these children think 24 hours a day, seven days a week. They feel that they are the few who know how to motivate these children, interpret for them, soothe them when they are emotionally hurt, and help them express their victories and defeats in acceptable ways. Difficult because as parents they feel like they are doing the educating, the care giving, the disciplining and completing the endless schoolwork assistance. Exhausting because every day and every week there are always things to do, things to finish (if you can get the child to acknowledge it has to be finished), and sometimes there is just no reasoning their way in or out of situations.

Parents say they worry constantly about their NLD child. Once their son was diagnosed one set of parents talked about their reluctance to accept the neurological issues of NLD. It took time and patience with themselves to accept that things needed to change for their son and he would reach his goals probably in different ways than his peers. His late diagnosis presented other issues that so many parents talked about: inadequate social skills. A very dedicated mother commented upon her son's high school graduation, "He thinks he doesn't need me anymore. I can't just walk away because he really needs me now more than ever!" Many parents felt that they have become the expert. Many parents report that one of the parents tends to be more patient than the other because they just have to be. Parents of students with NLD have had to learn to be proactive, thus providing a better form of special education or 504 services.

Sibling Relationships

Balance is important in families. The pressure of trying to meet the never ending needs of a child with NLD is certainly a family dynamic. Many families talked about the protective big brother or sister or friend. In many cases, they have assumed the role of social provider and protector. Siblings report they are sometimes embarrassed by their brother or sister in certain social settings, particularly school. They see the teasing and unfortunate harassment that takes place and are put into situations of fight or ignore. Siblings have a tough role to play with their family. Several families discussed the issues of younger siblings being the aggressor to the child with NLD and negative situations with that child. Children with NLD don't know how to fight fairly, so families report they band together and do lots of discussing and verbal communicating and practicing what to do in situations with all the children. Parents report that this has been invaluable for the entire family. It is unusual to find any family that does not report some sibling unrest. The NLD unrest is different and takes much longer to address, let alone solve.

The Early Years

Many parents report they knew something was wrong at a very early age and attempted to provide structure, compensatory strategies, punishment, or encouragement for whatever it was. Some parents carry guilt in not getting an early diagnosis. Other parents had the diagnosis, but felt unqualified and misunderstood to enlist the help their child needed. Parents report the signs were there all along, they just didn't know what they meant or how to deal. Perhaps what they saw was just their child's unique personality. Many agreed their child had some odd personality traits, but passed it off as just who they were. Some parents tell stories of very normal beginnings and no symptoms until late elementary school grades. These same parents now realize that perhaps what they saw as normal really wasn't.

Dr. Byron P. Rourke, a pioneer researcher in NLD, stresses the importance for families to find all the information, training, seminars, and diagnosis information they can. Parents say all of the information is available, but a stumbling block for some is the information that NLD is a neurologically based disability. Finding the right professional to interact with is vitally important. Many parents are overwhelmed at the testing information, and they report it takes them years to comprehend all of the technical information.

The Strengths and Challenges and What Works

All parents report that they see strengths in their children. They notice their intelligence, willingness to work hard, strong verbal skills, high interest and ability in reading, and efforts to be a good friend. Some children seem to have extraordinary gifts in the area of music or in working with animals. Others may have a keen interest in sports or other areas of leisure. They see students who want to be involved in the life of their school, however minimally that may be. A mother of a high school student reports her child doesn't realize there is anything wrong. When offered assistance, the answer is, " No, I am fine," when indeed it is not fine. There are tears over friends, explosions after school because of shear frustration, anxiety that prevents work from being completed, and often aggressive and volatile behavior. Parents report that most of these behaviors occur at home; however, the source for this level of stress is their school day.

Parents understand there are school issues and home issues. Often they become intertwined. When one is going well, it isn't unusual the other is showing signs of stress. Parents report that monthly school meetings help them interface with the staff working with their child. This regular schedule promotes an on-going working relationship that gives parents a basis of understanding and support. Only meeting when there is a crisis may encourage an adversarial relationship to form. It is important that all teachers and support personnel be involved in these meetings. The bus driver and the lunchroom staff need to know how to approach the student with NLD just as much as the science or math teacher. Many parents discuss their frustration that schools don't realize that everyone has to be trained. Suggestions by parents for in depth training have been well received in some schools and ignored in others.

The Impact of Early Diagnosis and School Interventions

Appropriate instruction for the student with NLD is important. Parents state that there is a varietability in the instruction their children receive. Much instruction has been outstanding and well thought out. Some instruction is adequate, but lacking in consistency and structure across the entire program. A few parents report they feel the schools have failed their children. With increased special education costs and a shortage of special education teachers, smaller school districts are paying a price. Resources appear to be the underlying cause for lack of programming; however, some small school communities have excellent programs. Parents reported caring, interest and concern of the professionals who drive their child's program.

Students diagnosed earlier appear to have an advantage in relation to services and programming. Developmentally, parents say they saw changes in social skills, some organization, physical developmental learning, conceptualizing (with cues), and more willingness to be involved in direct services of speech and language training, occupational therapy, and counseling. Research again points to early diagnosis and intervention being key to some success. Parents do talk about the acceptance of their children at a young age as opposed to late diagnosis and all the associated problems with NLD in middle school and high school.

Students diagnosed in middle school and high school face educational challenges, social difficulties, self-image issues, and a general lack of well being. Parents discussed not only the challenges of assisting their students at home with homework, but the role of social organizer for their child. Many parents get weary and feel they don't have the energy to sustain their child's needs.

A parent of a bright young women entering high school related the story of her child having lots of friends until sixth or seventh grade. Upon entering the middle grades, her child's social skills began eroding and friends weren't as tolerant. Even though they had known for a while that their friend was different, they abandoned her. Parents replaced peer time with their time, and fortunately the parents report older high school students have begun to be friends and supporters.

"It is so heart breaking to see your child go through this," a mother sadly reports. She continues, "NLD children don't have many friends. They are different and often get interpreted as weird. No one calls. No one invites them to go places. I understand why they get depressed." She continues to discuss the need for more social skill training and previewing events that are happening for NLD children. "Being a parent of an NLD child is exhausting! It just never stops. You think you have a solution and another problem arises. You always have to have your game face on with the world, and sometimes you are rejected by your own child for having the game face to begin with."

CHAPTER 4

Identification of Students with Nonverbal Learning Disabilities

Diagnosis

This chapter is rather short but concise because, in the author's opinion, there is a right way to diagnose NLD (best practice) and many less desirable and less accurate methods of diagnosing NLD. While compiling this chapter, it became clear that if we are going to best serve the student with NLD, we must give an accurate diagnosis. Only the most credible method will be reviewed—the 'gold standard' set out by Rourke et al (1989). Many schools, school psychologists, and special educators have diagnosed NLD, or a lack of NLD, using criteria based on hearsay, unreliable hand-me-down information, and urban legend. This is where many school districts falter and lose in mediation and due process hearings. There have been numerous times when our clinic has evaluated students who have been told they do not have NLD, when in fact they do (a false negative report), or that they have NLD, when in fact they do not (a false positive report). Several school districts around the country have set the criteria that a discrepancy of at least ten IQ points must exist on a Wechsler Intelligence Scale[1] (published by Harcourt Assessment Inc.) for a diagnosis of NLD to be made. Using this method is much akin to diagnosing a broken arm only by a physical examination and

---

[1] The Wechsler Intelligence Scale is available in three versions. A version is selected depending on the age of the individual to be tested.

without an x-ray. Yes, this method may be accurate in extreme cases, but it tends to miss the more frequent subtle cases.

Diagnostic Criteria

When looking at a diagnosis of NLD, a certain profile emerges on neuropsychological and cognitive testing. Individuals with the diagnosis typically exhibit impaired visual spatial functioning, visual working memory, tactile perception, perceptual abilities, fine and gross motor abilities, and higher order reasoning skills, with well preserved language functioning (Rourke, 1989). There are eight characteristics that Rourke has developed when assessing individuals with NLD and they are as follows[2]:

1) Performance on the Target Test falls one standard deviation below the mean (90);
2) No or very minimal simple tactile imperceptions and suppressions versus very poor finger agnosia, finger dysgraphesthesia, and astereognosis composite (90);
3) Two of Wechsler Vocabulary, Similarities, and Information subtests are the highest of the Verbal scales (76):
4) Two of Wechsler Block Design, Object Assembly, and Coding subtests are the lowest of the Performance scales (76):
5) Academic achievement in Reading is at least eight points greater than Arithmetic (72);
6) Tactual Performance Test Right, Left, and Both hand times become progressively worse vis-à-vis norms (66);
7) Normal to superior grip strength versus mildly to moderately impaired Grooved Pegboard (59);
8) Wechsler VIQ > PIQ at least ten points (41)

---

[2] The numbers in parentheses represent the percent of individuals with NLD who are identified with that particular test.

The diagnostic criteria related to the eight characteristics are as follows:

If the first 5 features are present:	Definite NLD
If 7 or 8 of these 8 features are present:	Definite NLD
If 5 or 6 of these 8 features are present:	Probable NLD
If 3 or 4 of these 8 features are present:	Questionable NLD
If 1 or 2 of these 8 features are present:	Low Probability of NLD

What should be noted with the above criteria is that all of the tests listed above are given as part of a battery of tests (i.e., the Halstead-Reitan Neuropsychological Battery—also known as the HRB, 1993). While there are several other methods that have support in diagnosing NLD, the majority of research that was conducted has utilized the HRB.

Special Education and Neuropsychological Findings

When considering obtaining a neuropsychological evaluation for a student that you suspect has NLD, it is important to interview the neuropsychologist as to their experience in the field, the instruments they typically use and are comfortable with, and their understanding of NLD. While there are multiple methods of conducting a neuropsychological evaluation, it is important to obtain one that will answer your diagnostic questions and provide objective data that will support the recommendations.

Again, the HRB is the recommended battery. One of the greatest struggles that schools repeatedly experience is the disconnect between what the neuropsychologist finds to be useful and puts in their reports and what the school can use and needs to appropriately support the student with NLD while at the same time meeting their legal mandate to find the student eligible for special education under Individuals with Disabilities Education Act (IDEA, 2004), accommodations under Section 504 of the American with Disabilities Act (ADA, 1990), or other regional supports that are sanctioned by the state government or the local Local Educational Agency (LEA). Both schools and parents need to be willing to have a frank discussion regarding their separate needs. Below are some suggested questions that are best asked of the neuropsychologist when contemplating a neuropsychological evaluation as well as a suggested evaluation battery. This list is not exhaustive and can be added to.

Does have a Nonverbal Learning Disability according to the diagnostic criteria put forward by Dr. Byron Rourke?

What are this student's cognitive abilities?

What are this student's strengths?

What are this student's challenges?

What are this student's current life circumstances?

What is the nature/extent of exceptional life circumstances on 's learning and school functioning?

What are this student's levels of adaptive behavioral functioning?

What are this student's behavioral, emotional, and social characteristics?

Is there a discrepancy greater than 1.5 standard deviations below the expected achievement level for 's ability level that is not the result of a visual, hearing, or motor disability; learning impairment; emotional disturbance; or environmental, cultural, or economic disadvantage?

The following is a list of *suggested* evaluation instruments for the neuropsychological evaluation that could answer the above questions:

Classroom/School Observation
Structured Student Interview
School Cumulative Record Folder review
Developmental History
Parent Interview
Teacher Interview

Interview with pertinent health professionals (physicians, psychologists, social workers, etc.)

(one of the following according to age)
    Wechsler Intelligence Scale for Children—IV
    Wechsler Adult Intelligence Scale-III
    Wechsler Preschool and Primary Scales of Intelligence—III

Rey-Osterrieth Complex Figure Test and/or the Beery-Buktenica Developmental Test of Visual-Motor Integration

A measure of academic achievement such as the Wechsler Individual Achievement Test—II, or the Woodcock-Johnson Achievement Battery, as well as at least one separate test or written expression such as the Test of Written Language.

The Halstead Reitan Neuropsychological Battery that could include:
    Children's Category Test—Level 1/2
    Sentence Memory/Repetition Test
    Revised Knox Cube Test
    Seashore Rhythm Test
    Speech-Sounds Perception Test
    Verbal Fluency Test
    Auditory Closure Test
    Progressive Figures Test
    Trail Making Test
    Grooved Pegboard Test
    Finger Oscillation (Tapping) Test
    Name Writing Test
    Lateral Preference Test
    Sensory-Perceptual Examination
    Aphasia Screening Examination
    Tactual Performance Test
    Dynamic Grip Strength Test

Target Test

Wide Range Assessment of Memory and Learning

A measure of self-esteem such as the Self-Esteem Inventory

A measure of anxiety such as the Revised Children's Manifest Anxiety Scale and/or the Multidimensional Anxiety Scale for Children

A measure of depression such as the Reynolds Child Depression Scale, the Reynolds Adolescent Depression Scale, or the Kovacs' Children's Depression Inventory

A measure of personality (no projective techniques) such as Personality Inventory for Youth, the Minnesota Multiphasic Personality Inventory for Adolescents, the Minnesota Multiphasic Personality Inventory—2, and/or the Personality Inventory for Children.

And lastly, a measure of adaptive behavioral functioning such as the AAMR Adaptive Behavior Scale—School Form, the Vineland Adaptive Behavior Scales, and/or the Adaptive Behavior Assessment System—Parent and Teacher Forms.

CHAPTER 5

The Role of the Special Educator

Developing a Working Relationship with Students with NLD

Learning Disabled (LD) students in their adolescent years work to develop an understanding and responsibility for their learning style. Goals at this point move from special educator centered programming, where development of skills and coping strategies provides the basis of student/teacher work, to a model where students start to manage their work completion, to regulate their study time, and to develop their own system for facilitating their independent work.

When a student with NLD is asked to operate student-centered expectations, disaster can be eminent. The concept that adolescents need to begin to internalize feelings of independence and a system of natural consequences works well with most at this developmental stage. How does it feel when grades reflect the investment of personal time and academic energies? What can happen when work is submitted late or not at all? The ability to have an accurate self-reflection is also present to a limited extent for students with a nonverbal learning disability.

Self-regulation or self-monitoring continues to be an externalized need for students with NLD. Their perceptions of the academic world do not always equate with those of educators. This view of their learning environment ranges from how students and teachers see them, to what is expected in their daily classes, or how they are achieving academically. Often these students have little confidence as to the goal of the daily assignments, whether there are any long-term projects, and if they are moving in the right direction to progress in each class. The expectations and systems for each class may vary so greatly that a student with NLD may be content to just have negotiated the period-to-period schedule. (It can only be hoped that there were no assemblies, meetings with school counselors, or other adaptations to the schedule, which would make this predictable schedule run amuck.)

One of the first goals of a special educator in working with a student with NLD is to make the unpredictable world of school appear predictable. Providing a daily structure in a system known for its' "flexibility" allows students with NLD to begin to map out their role in this over stimulating environment. In the middle and high school settings, this can be extremely challenging with block schedule models and vacillating timetables that allow for creativity of thought and dynamic groupings.

Students with NLD need to have the script of the school day ahead of time. It allows them to know the end of the story without reading the book. Predicting the possible outcomes of their day is a game they often lose. This begins with the order of the academics, the teachers that they will be asked to interact with, and may include what will be covered in their classes. Starting each day with the special educator can provide the setting for this to occur. Once the student maneuvers the hallways to get to the resource room, going through an overview of the day would alleviate a great number of fears. This time also provides an opportunity to review for accuracy work that had been assigned in these classes, and to establish goals for new work to be accomplished.

Addressing the fears of inaccurate perceptions allows the learner with NLD to be ready for the information being presented in class. This predictable format not only impacts their success in negotiating the daily schedule, but also provides a consistent format for new information storage. The system of recording class work, organizing new materials, and understanding each teacher's style, further addresses the learning style of students with NLD.

As a special educator in a middle and high school, this seemingly invasive role is contrary to the usual plan for intervention. Not only must the special educator provide an external structure or framework for the student's day, but he or she must also use this approach with other aspects of the student's program. This includes the student's personal system of organization. The student's backpack must be unzipped, the papers extracted, and the binders reviewed. Once again, the student with NLD will be grateful that they were able to move from class to class and have few uncomfortable social interactions. By the end of the day, the student's organization system is often nonexistent or at least in disarray.

Again at this developmental stage, educators feel the need for each student to develop a system of collecting papers, recording assignments, and identifying work to be completed. This is not the case for students with NLD; the systems must be imposed. The student's backpack needs to be opened daily, the binders reviewed to include a predictable system of organization, and the assignment book completed for accuracy. Each class must have its own three ringed binder with identified sections. The first section is work to be turned in to teachers during the next class. The student with NLD needs to have one place to check for all completed work. Searching for homework at the start of class only intensifies the level of anxiety. The next section in the binder is current coursework. It contains those items that the teacher will expect the student to be familiar with and have easy access to, such as class notes, any long term projects or readings, and work that may be included in an upcoming test. This section is then followed by any past daily assignments or readings. This system allows for easy access when preparing for long-term exams. The final section includes completed assessments. This may include graded long-term projects, quizzes or chapter tests. Not only does this provide opportunities for review, but allows the student with NLD to more accurately view his or her personal progress in the class.

While working on a daily basis with the student with NLD, the role of a special educator focuses on providing an external framework that does not naturally exist. This scaffolding, both for maintaining a predictable schedule and a system for acquiring knowledge, addresses the lack of internalized structure. Providing this structure allows students with NLD to begin to achieve academically at a level commensurate with their ability.

Facilitating Success in the School Environment

Another important role of the special educator with the student with NLD is that of liaison to other educators. Often these students' behavior in the classroom and school, as well as their functioning in the classroom, is so contrary to other students that educators misread these actions. It is the role of the special educator during these opportunities to educate others in the building as to why students with NLD perform in this way.

Classroom teachers and school counselors often perceive students with NLD characteristics in the classroom to be a behavioral issue. Students with nonverbal learning disabilities need to observe social interactions, their role in student groups, and their interactions with teachers. Often these interactions can reveal symptoms of depression, oppositional defiance, or general immaturity. While students with NLD can be incredibly verbal and engaged during class time, they often produce little written output either during class or for homework. Regular educators can construe this to mean that they are lazy, avoiding work, or not engaged in the class. Their verbal strengths allow them to demonstrate to educators that they are highly competent individuals. Their scores on short objective tests may reinforce this belief for educators. But quickly this perception is questioned, when long term assignments never appear, when essays continue to be a laborious activity, and when these activities compiled result in failing grades for the student.

The special educator at this time becomes the consultant. While the Individual Education Plan may clearly outline the strengths and needs of these students, the varied nature of the academic performance may bring into question the accuracy of this document. Special educators must then educate regular classroom teachers, school counselors and administrators as to why these behaviors can be a result of this disability.

Classroom teachers need to understand the difference between verbal output and academic production. The challenges these students have in organizing and producing those brilliant ideas, that so easily come when spoken in class, are not obvious to teachers. Often these students can provide some of the most accurate and detailed contributions in a classroom discussion. They can make connections to previously covered material and reflect to the teacher what was presented in readings and lectures. While their responses may lack abstract thought, the content is strong enough so that teachers can assess a high level of competency and understanding. What confuses the teacher, however, is when other assessments never appear.

The concept that was easily articulated in class does not result in the short answer assignment that was given for homework. The long-term project that was discussed in class, reviewed individually with the teacher, and had short term goals established, cannot be found. What is also important to note here is that these students can be masterful in convincing teachers that all is well. In their need to please adults and manage their academic anxieties, they are able to convince educators that the work is at home (on a different disk than the one they have) and is all under their control. Days after the due date, it is obvious that there is no work and by then even more work is due. It is the role of the special educator to anticipate these trappings and to provide other educators with the information so they can see where the challenges are for the student with NLD.

School counselors must learn that these students' rigidity in the hallway and challenged personal interactions are a result of perceptual challenges. Developing a predictable format for interactions and an accepting style will allow these students to be themselves and more available. Again, these students attempt to present that all is well, meanwhile their anxiety level is increasing. The ability to describe feelings and connect them to emotions is challenging for students with NLD. The role of the special educator in working with the school counselor is both to provide an overview of this student's style and to assist the student in accessing this resource.

Special educators can provide counselors and students with the structure that allow these interactions to be more successful. In working with the student, they need to know what will be expected of them in this setting, how most counseling appointments are structured, and what may be asked of them. Scripting possible conversations without limiting the content of their discussions is possible. First meetings should focus on simple concepts where the student has a clear agenda. This could be course selection or interviewing the school counselor about what their job entails. It is helpful for students with NLD to have a clear understanding of what each educator's job at school is and how the educator may be helpful to them. In other words, who is the expert of what.

The school counselor has an important expertise that is valuable both to the student with NLD and to the special educator. In later meetings with the school counselor, more sensitive issues can be discussed if needed. Once the student with NLD has an understanding of the counselor's role, a familiarity as to the structure and setting of appointments, and a script for conversation initiation, discussions of fears and concerns regarding school should occur more easily. This process is also true in working with therapeutic counselors. Special educators have the responsibility for informing these professionals of the challenges and strengths of students with NLD. With this information, the school counselor can be an additional resource to the student and his/her team.

Administrators also have a need to know what is important for them to emphasize in their work with students with NLD.

Those individuals in the school who are responsible for addressing student behavior and in facilitating a student's program outside the classroom have a unique challenge in working with these students. Their interactions may not be as consistent as other professionals in the building. The student may be accessing them to address concerns of interactions with other students, or they may be directed to the office as a result of their own behaviors. Here a scripted process can be helpful. The special educator may be initially invited to sessions with administrators as a mediator or support person.

As a result of their high verbal skills, the point of the initial contact with the administrator may be quickly lost. The student with NLD may demonstrate a quick increase in anxiety when working with a "new" member of the school team. Scripts for addressing behavioral issues can be as simple as using the same specific questions in each student/administrator interaction. What happened? What was your role? Who was involved? This allows the student to begin to frame a response prior to the interaction. Once the script is in place, the administrator then needs to manage the response so that it only includes the key information. Again, this student's language abilities can produce long and convoluted answers that can lengthen the interview to the point that it is nonproductive. The role of the special educator is to provide administrators with these tools in advance of possible interactions. This allows for greater probability for a successful interaction.

The final critical member of any educational team is the parent. Parents need to be effective participants in the planning and development of their child's program. For any parent of a child with a disability believing that the school is going to meet their child's individual needs can be challenging. This is especially true for parents of a student with NLD. The process employed to correctly identify their son or daughter as having a nonverbal learning disability may have been long and arduous. All along they knew that their child learned and socialized differently. Time and again they saw their child not succeed to the level that the parent knew he or she could. Eventually, testing may have occurred, but no evident disability was found. Over time and with perseverance on the parent's part, the appropriate determination was made. They are then asked to trust the school team to provide the right program.

Being a constant source for feedback and a resource for information are common expectations for special educators. In working with families of students with NLD, the goals of these parents expand beyond the school day, and the application of a consistent system of addressing these needs is extremely important. The structure and scripts that have been addressed earlier also need to be in place at home. Educators are comfortable shifting their approaches based on student needs. Parents have greater challenges in relearning their parenting style and varying it from child to child in their own home. While parents of other students with disabilities may obviously know that traditional systems of parenting cannot work with their child, this is less easily seen with a child with NLD. This child's verbal strengths trap parents into believing that all of their competencies are at the same superior level. Parental expectations may not then coincide with their true capabilities.

Further, parents provide meaningful information to the school team about what has worked with their child. The successes and growth that they have seen is valuable information. Also, home is the one place that these children often feel at ease. Their parents may be the only people that they can trust with their true feelings and perceptions.

As the liaison between home and school, the special educator needs to be available to parents' concerns, to use the parents as a resource of information, and to assist the parent in understanding the nature of their child's disability. When parents read the literature on nonverbal learning disabilities, they will need assistance to see how this information relates to their child and understand that each step in their child's academic program will be impacted by the child's learning needs. This includes each and every transition from elementary to middle school, from middle to high school, and from high school to post secondary plans. Issues that were believed to be resolved, in terms of familiarity with educational and social systems, will arise with each change on the horizon. Until their child arrives at a point in life where all systems are predictable, possibly with the right career choice, there will be important obstacles for the family to negotiate, and the special educator plays a critical role in maneuvering through these challenges.

Special educators have a variety of responsibilities in working with students with NLD that may challenge their concept of their role. The level of structure needed to create a productive learning environment is greatly increased. The evasive nature of their interactions, not allowing these students to hide under any stone and in any way, can be uncomfortable. The quantity of information that needs to be shared with a variety of school members and family may seem daunting. Each of these roles, however, can assist in creating a constructive environment for students with NLD so that eventually they can begin to internalize these systems of instruction. As they become more comfortable with their learning styles and the school setting, they will develop into more independent learners and will be able to identify where they need help.

Needs Based Programming

The term "needs based programming" describes the process used to determine the kinds and quantity of services a student may receive. The process puts the student at the center of decision-making. Rather than looking at a menu of services that are available within the school environment, the team focuses on the strengths and challenges of each individual student. All students would benefit from a team of professional interventionists. However, the amount of time that a student is separated from his or her peers and is outside the regular learning environment is an equal factor in determining services. When the right accommodations are in place and the regular educator is aware of the student's learning profile, the traditional classroom environment is an important part in the student's IEP. Looking at the specific needs and qualities of the student can alleviate the amount of time a student is pulled away from that setting.

Not all students with NLD fit into a tight and predictable mold for service needs. As is found in all disabilities, students with NLD can have a range of needs and varied strengths. The first step in the process in having an appropriate match between needs and programming is to have a comprehensive psychological evaluation. Strong test data can determine the diversity of their cognitive abilities, the extent to which cognitive needs have impacted their ability to acquire information in the classroom, and the emotional issues that may have arisen as a result of their difficulties with social perceptions.

Once a baseline is determined, comparing this information with the observations and experiences of the members of the school team is the next step. While testing data provides the team with a view of the student in isolation, the collective knowledge of the school team adds depth to these statistics. How these strengths and challenges translate into the day-to-day interactions of this child is critical. Collection of this anecdotal data further enhances the picture of the student.

Needs based programming dictates that the program put in place responds to the severity of the disability. Students with NLD may only require the daily structure of access to the special educator to assist with organization and planning. This service, in conjunction with appropriate classroom accommodations may be the extent of their individual education plan along with the established program goals.

A more intensive needs student with NLD may require a more comprehensive program. This could include daily meetings with the special educator for assistance with organization systems, development of personal scripts for social interaction, specific skill development in math and reading comprehension, and social skills training. In addition, the IEP may include a detailed behavior plan, which outlines the roles and responsibilities of the school team and the expectations for the student's responses. More intensive needs students with NLD may also have as part of their plan an extensive list of classroom accommodations. This list allows the student to achieve at a level commensurate with his or her ability while respecting the core content of the class. Accommodations that address out of classroom assignments and assessment strategies are critical for this student's success. Finally, this student may need a range of related service providers including a speech/language pathologist, individual therapist, and/or behavioral consultant who bring the specialized instruction and intervention that each student may need.

Having the student at the center of this decision-making process ensures that the appropriate combination of intervention and skill development, as well as access to the regular education setting, is in place. The special educator who facilitates this process ensures the balance between the two sides of this equation. Without participation in the traditional classroom, these students will be led to believe that they can only successfully operate in small one-on-one settings. The right program will allow them to expand their worlds to include greater numbers of people and a broader range of experiences.

Choosing the Right Services, Not All of the Services

The continuum of service needs for students with NLD can be incredibly diverse. The Individual Education Plan (IEP) team identifies which services are necessary. The role of the special educator is to facilitate that decision-making process to ensure that the appropriate services are chosen. Using the right questions to focus the team assists the special educator in that process.

All students can benefit from a collaborative educational plan that includes a range of interventional experts. However, the amount of direct instruction time with their peers is compromised when they are removed from the regular classroom to receive services. The balance between specialized instruction and access to a normalized environment is an important consideration.

Asking the team specific clarifying questions can assist the team in finding the right combination of services and access. Instead of looking at what the student would benefit from, the team should be asked what the student needs in order to succeed at a level commensurate with peers of the same age. When looking at benefit as opposed to need, the list of services can be endless. In contrast, the idea of need focuses on addressing the specific challenges of the child and on providing the skills necessary to participate in the regular classroom at a level comparable to peers of the same age. This allows the appropriate access to the regular classroom.

Not only must the team determine which services would provide appropriate access, it must also prioritize service needs. While the team begins to narrow its view, there still may remain an extensive number of interventions that need to occur. Ranking these services by their importance by allowing the student access to their education further focuses the team. In addition, as some educational needs are addressed other issues may be corrected. Triaging educational needs looks at which interventions will have the greatest impact on the student's ability to be successful at that particular time.

Though the student may benefit from social skills training, for example, addressing the student's level of anxiety in academic settings by providing a highly structured learning environment may be the first step. The predictable setting may alone address issues of socialization and ease in the classroom. Identifying first steps also allows the special educator to further diagnosis the root sources of some learning problems. The impact of a student's anxieties in the school may repress many skills such as written output or abstract thought. Addressing the anxiety level first lets the special educator see the true potential of the student.

One approach to ensuring that the right services are chosen is to begin with identifying the individualized goals for the student. The team must answer the questions where do we want the student to be in a year's time, and what is the greatest obstacle to that progress? By answering these two questions on the goal page of the IEP, the team is identifying the first steps towards academic growth for this child.

The first question incorporates a number of issues. First, the team must have an understanding of the potential progress this student can make in a year. Team members will have assumptions about the student's probability for growth based on prior experience. Looking at the amount of time that was needed to introduce and solidify the student's understanding of new concepts in prior learning situations helps to determine the number of goals that can be successfully addressed in an individual plan.

Second, the team needs to discuss what goals it has for the student. Each team member walks into the room with an agenda. The parents may see the ability to socialize and integrate with peers as priority. The regular educator may wish to enhance the student's ability to submit class work in a timely manner. The special educator sees the need to increase written output. These goals have similar intents in improving academic success and may all be a part of the student's plan. Discussing each member's perspective in setting goals ensures that everyone has a say in the development of the educational plan.

The second question focuses the team as to which of the student's current behaviors are getting in the way of these goals. Generating the list of goals based on team observations and evaluation data can produce any number of goals. Using the benchmark of obstacles asks the team to look further at the root sources of some academic behaviors. Timely submission of academic work may become an issue as the student does not have a well-organized system for work completion and submission. The student may also have difficulties in clarifying the intent of an assignment when it is presented in class. Taking each general goal and determining why this is not currently occurring breaks the process of intervention into meaningful objective steps.

By knowing the right questions to ask and focusing the IEP

team in its decision-making, the special educator is fulfilling a critical role by working with a student with NLD. Having a productive and constructive IEP team contributes to the special educator's probability of success in addressing the student's needs. Using a questioning process to facilitate these discussions allows every member the opportunity to share a perspective of the child and agenda in the meeting. Being heard as a parent, classroom teacher or service provider validates the importance of team membership. The special educator sets the tone and the structure to these meetings that can allow this to occur.

In summary, the role of the special educator in working with students with nonverbal learning disabilities differs from his or her previous work in many ways. Special educators are asked to facilitate the integration of these students into a world very foreign to them. Each possible interaction for a student with NLD needs to be considered and appropriate responses planned. Once team members are aware of the needs of these students, they must then have the opportunity to make informed decisions that develop the student's IEP.

Taking a highly structured and directive stance may be more comfortable for some special educators who work with younger students. However, this is not the typical posture for interventionists with developmentally older students. It may at times feel authoritarian and dictatorial, but it does provide the predictable environment that these students relish.

The student is armed with a greater sense of control of their learning environment once systems and structure are in place and are part of the daily routine. Systems include how their day is structured, previews of upcoming events, an organized approach for collection and storing of class work, and scripts for possible personal interactions. Tools such as these provide the predictability that students with NLD need and desire.

With the atmosphere in the resource room established, the special educator then must direct his or her attention to the role of working with the other members of the IEP team. The special educator lays the groundwork for the student's potential for success throughout the school building. Informing all members of the skills and challenges of students with NLD, as well as planning for possible difficulties, increases the probability that the student will feel comfortable and accepted in the school. Providing the training, and discussing the impact of these challenges, allows all team members, from teachers to administrators, counselors to parents, the information necessary to understand the issues of students with NLD.

A well-versed and prepared team is the first step in the development of a constructive decision-making process. The special educator is the facilitator of this process. In this role, he or she must again lay the structure for possible success. Asking those questions that look to the root needs of the student with NLD provides the framework for this to occur. The special educator must also consider the perspective of all team members and allow for discussion of their goals. Facilitating the team, rather than directing the decisions, allows all members to feel that they have had a hand in molding the student's individual program.

While a special educator is asked to retool his or her role as an interventionist, many of these skills are aleady in place. Being a good communicator, planning for possible outcomes, understanding the nature of the disability, and constructing productive educational teams have long been part of the special education profession. The extensive nature of this program is more reflective of students who have greater cognitive and physical needs. Though students with nonverbal learning disabilities may blend in with their academic peers in some ways, their needs are complex. The special educator provides the structure and the systems necessary for these students to interact more effectively.

CHAPTER 6

Regular Education Teachers' Perspectives of Students with Nonverbal Learning Disabilities (NLD)

The Role of the Regular Educator

The regular educator plays a key role in working with the student with Nonverbal Learning Disabilities. While the goal of all teachers is to impart their expertise in their subject area and inspire their students, the current increase in special education students within the classroom presents its own set of challenges. Teachers are being asked to do more in their classes, particularly with these students. They see accommodations and modifications as unrealistic—not in their expertise—and way beyond what they signed on to do. Most often teachers commented that they knew nothing about NLD or that they felt behind in learning ways to help their students. Of course there were also the naysayers. They often reported they felt this was a "fad" diagnosis. Fortunately, most teachers see all students as capable learners in the educational community until facts and evidence of learning is proven differently. Teachers discussed their challenges of teaching students with Nonverbal Learning Disabilities openly and candidly for this book.

For the student with NLD, the teacher's role is established from the moment class begins or even in a perchance meeting in the hall. It might be the color of the teacher's hair, the tone of his or her voice, the set up of the room, or the fact that "Tony bugs me" and he is in this class. It is important to remember that the NLD perspective is everything. Once it is established, it is very tough to rearrange the perspective. Perspective is often so inaccurate that the student is oblivious to the inaccuracy. Remember that one of the most inhibiting factors of NLD is the ability to interpret what the student sees and processes multi-modally. Thus it would be easy for a relationship to go bad with the first encounter. Fortunately, with good preparation for the classroom teacher from the special educator this need not happen. Special educators must arrive early before school begins or following a diagnosis. They must review the needs of these students with the team of educators interacting daily with the student.

Teachers' Understanding of Students with NLD

Teachers report their frustrations regarding a real understanding of this disability. They certainly understand Down Syndrome and associated severe genetic or birth trauma disorders. Attention deficit categories can be generalized, and a learning disability in math or reading can be understood and dealt with adequately in a classroom. The NLD profile is, however, unique for each student.

Generally, these students have average to above average intelligent quotients. Teachers look at those scores and have difficulty understanding the challenges. The right brain dysfunction can't be seen and often the student covers for the disability quite well. Teachers have reported their students seem a little different. They are left out, don't make appropriate social comments, or worse, are the blunt of behind-the-back jokes from their peers.

Students with NLD will openly acknowledge that they understand everything that is being imparted in the classroom, and that the teacher often has problems seeing the challenges right away. The first missing homework assignments are acknowledged as being at home or on the computer. The teacher who waits can find a grading period well under way with NO assignments turned in to them. Many of the teachers we spoke to relate that they have, in many instances, learned by doing! Good preparation and follow up are key in working with the teaching team. Teachers tell us that they appreciate weekly check-ins by the special educator or direct service provider. Many teachers discussed how homework checklists, weekly reporting systems, weekly meetings, email, and other communication systems are extremely helpful in keeping a good inventory of work production for their NLD students. Teachers also commented that they find themselves setting unrealistic goals for students with NLD. They want multiple written products done to their specifications. Often, the teachers report that they get no written product. After this has occurred many times, they begin to realize that the student with NLD is organizationally challenged and lacks initiation.

How Some Teachers Have Learned About NLD

Teachers report that working with students with NLD can be both trying and rewarding. To the best of their ability, they want to understand, learn, and teach their students. This can pose a challenge since some teachers report class sizes of 25–30 students. Skills learned from working with a student with NLD will benefit all students. The strategies teachers report work best for them are ones they also report benefit all students. They do not discount the importance of individualizing the curriculum for students with NLD.

Teachers report they find it helpful to dialogue with special educators regarding this disability. They say they often feel inadequate and need step-by-step definitions and teaching strategies to assist them. A weekly meeting for ten to fifteen minutes will provide excellent support and often turns into a longer session.

Many teachers have found self-research helpful. They take the initiative to tap the technology resources available and begin reading. If you find there isn't that initiative, it is helpful to draw from the notable resources on NLD. Some special educators develop their own short lists to share with their teachers during their weekly meetings. A list a week is very effective and not intimidating.

An IEP At-A-Glance has reportedly been useful for some special educators. It allows the information to be presented in a one page document that is easy to digest and lists the very pertinent information regarding the IEP student. This is used in conjunction with the complete IEP.

Teachers comment that it is productive if initial meetings focus on building a team philosophy. The special educator assists the teacher in understanding the strengths and challenges of the individual student. In working with teams, it has been found that building a working relationship can take one month, six months, or even a year. As the relationship grows, teachers report they reach a "comfort level" and can work with the special educator on accommodations and modifications.

Positive Outcomes for Teachers and Their Students

Teachers say that they have often been overwhelmed with the expectations of what has to be done to assist the student with NLD. Varying assessments, modifying assignments, and learning how to discuss topics with their students are listed as the most problematic issues with teachers.

Teachers who find multiple and creative ways of assessment report they appear to have outstanding rapport with their students with NLD. The first assessment session is usually interesting as they learn to listen to the verbal output of their students. After discussions regarding assessment, one teacher of an extremely bright student with NLD decided to alter his testing and include assessment during in informal conversation with his student. He reported his amazement at the depth of course material understanding the student displayed and the student's ability to process back to his teacher his knowledge verbally.

At a team meeting this same teacher recounted that this student had some of the best synthesis skills in his class. The student was a great contributor to class discussions, and his peers respected what he had to say. Initially, this teacher was going to require written notes on films and class presentations. Upon learning the pitfalls (classic shut down and not hearing the lecture) involved in requiring such accountability, the teacher used peers notes for the student. Recently, this teacher has begun to copy his own class notes from his lectures. His feeling was that his teaching notes were the best, and this student deserved the best. Furthermore, the teacher would know the student received what was actually being given in class for review. This teacher really benefited from the close working relationship of the special educator.

Observations of educators working with students with NLD reveal they become more aware of teaching techniques that are helpful through modeling. In many cases, having an expert in NLD work directly with teachers has proven to be invaluable. Teachers are willing to ask questions—let the expert practice with them—and most importantly help them shift some of their teaching paradigms. The expert can be a special educator, a consultant, another teacher, or a parent. Intervention is necessary and the school team has a responsibility to meet this student's needs.

Many teachers report they don't think the total needs of these students are being met because of lack of intervention understanding. Accommodations and modifications are often challenged as a change in the course material and content, thus altering the credibility and efficacy of the course. It takes a fine balance of expertise and credibility to meet the needs of the student with NLD. In discussions with teachers their willingness to accommodate is evident; however, their willingness to understand that less is more is a conflict.

Many teachers have reported the accommodations that work best for them are those of sensible nature. They also report the need to limit the number of team members a teacher has to interact with regarding this student. They need an expert they can go to when problems arise. Teachers understand the need to break down long term assignments, but they sometimes forget that it is next to impossible for the student with NLD to complete every step. Working with a student with NLD is a daily function, not a biweekly review. Most teachers find it cumbersome to do the daily checks that need to be done to keep NLD students on top of their work. There is a mentality that you are in high school and you have responsibilities for your work. Fortunately, teachers report they have great success with NLD students when they are working daily with them, even if it is a brief conversation and visual connect with the work.

All teachers unanimously agree that grading is the most difficult task they have. Interviews with teachers indicate some, not all, can't adjust their grading systems. They have difficulty with the old quantity versus quality issue. With continued support teachers slowly begin to understand the depth of challenges these students have with work completion. One teacher reported she liked to look at the continuum of knowledge her student had acquired while in her classroom. She acknowledged that although all assignments were not complete, what was complete was the general working knowledge her student with NLD had acquired, processed and synthesized. She was delighted she had been able to assess the student's working knowledge in the beginning of the course and continue to assess the grandness of that knowledge by the end of the course. This teacher discussed the difficulty she had in getting to that final assessment. Her accountability to the content of the course haunted her. Also, her accountability to the grading system of the school was ever present in her mind. Most importantly was her sincere sense of accountability to the student for assessment, understanding of the NLD disability, and tailoring her teaching to meet those paramount needs on a daily basis. Both the teacher and the student were winners in this equation.

Teachers consistently comment about the tenacity and drive the parents of students with NLD have. Some teachers have reported the parents have helped them understand more about their student than anyone else. Acknowledging the parent role from a teacher's point of view is sometimes a bit difficult. These parents may not be driven for top level university admissions; mostly, they want to extend their working knowledge to the school regarding their child. They want the best education their child can receive, and most often acknowledge they know it isn't easy to teach their youngster. Often they are the interpreters of the world for their student.

Parents are often a little different in their approaches to teachers. They are bright, well informed, well educated on the disability, and know just about every way to approach their child for school work. They belong to parent networks and interface with other parents via the internet or school. They are the resident experts! They will be the first cheering team for the teachers, as long as needs are being met.

Not all parents meet this profile. Denial is often a culprit for parents and that stands in the way of success and failure. Parents get burned out on homework, structure, world interpretation, social isolation for their child, and are often the blame when lack of progress is thrown at the school and the teachers. It takes listening, creativity on the part of the IEP team, and patience to work with this small portion of the parent NLD population. A school must have a philosophy for its teachers and staff and stand by that philosophy. Often the school is expected to meet the ongoing needs of everything related to NLD, and that is indeed unrealistic. Through coordinated teaming and good listening skills a school team can survive the negative parent. (See Chapter 12 on Team Building.) A good mantra to recite is, "Each team member has expertise to bring to this student— through hard work they can and will meet the needs of his/her education."

CHAPTER 7

Emotional Issues Related to Nonverbal Learning Disabilities (NLD)

Typical Emotional Development

While they appear verbally bright, individuals with NLD have inherent difficulty with higher order reasoning and problem solving abilities, visual spatial and organizational abilities, and understanding nonverbal language of social interactions.

Students with NLD have typically moved through several diagnostic categories as they grew older (See Chart). Initially, very young children with NLD may be identified as potentially hearing impaired because of their lack of eye contact or seeming lack of reaction to auditory information. They are frequently screened for their hearing and seen by hearing specialists. Once that diagnosis is set aside, and prior to the development of language, the issue of Autism is raised to explain their idiosyncratic behaviors. This diagnosis is usually substituted by well meaning diagnosticians for Pervasive Developmental Disorder—Not otherwise Specified (PDD-NOS) once the child has starting talking and does not stop. This diagnosis may be fine tuned once they sample his language—especially in light of the special interests and nonstop discussion about topics that typically make them anxious. Children with NLD typically over-talk about what is making them nervous or about a subject that offers them a sense of mastery in an attempt at self-soothing. This rarely works since talking about what makes them anxious just increases their anxiety, and talking about what they know, while offering mild temporary relief, does not target the anxiety producing issue. These behaviors tend to lead to diagnosis of Obsessive-Compulsive Disorder (OCD) since many times these children may also develop rituals to accompany their over-talk. What must be kept in mind is that these behaviors do not represent any intrapsychic conflict (as seen in the television show Monk or for those slightly older—Felix Unger from the Odd Couple) but feeble attempts to self-sooth and reduce anxiety. As one adolescent student with NLD put it, "I worry about if I'm worrying about the right things . . . I don't know what to worry about!" When accommodations are appropriately put in place, OCD symptoms become less apparent, and the need for these behaviors diminishes.

Students with NLD also usually begin to display anxiety in the early elementary grades. As students enter middle school, these problems intensify and generalize to multiple areas of their life. Many students begin to withdraw from both school and family, choosing to spend as much time as possible in their bedrooms because they find comfort in that environment. If they have a telephone, television, a computer, and internet connection available, many students isolate themselves in a self-preservation type of behavior. Whenever they are forced to emerge, their anxiety rises and they report feeling overwhelmed and out of control. These feelings of hopelessness and helplessness often develop into depression and a greater potential for suicide.

As one parent put it, "I am the chief interpreter of the world for my child." Parents need to recognize that they will often be told that they are overprotective; however, school personnel need to recognize that the parents have been witness to an extended history of subtle and not so subtle abuse of their child by others, especially in the school setting. As a result of this close relationship, children with NLD will have a very difficult time separating from their parents as is expected in adolescence. One of two things typically happens, either the emergence of the adolescent occurs with great trepidation on the part of both the parent and child (often accompanied by much anger and derision), or separation does not happen at all, leaving the child tied to the parents often until their mid twenties to early thirties.

A study (Rourke, 1988) was conducted over several years investigating the relationship between neurotypical individuals, individuals with a language based learning disability (e.g., dyslexia), and individuals with NLD. What Rourke found was that NLD exhibits more clinical and more internalized forms of psychopathology than individuals with language based learning disabilities and neurotypical individuals. They also found that, while individuals with a language-based learning disability may have emotional problems during school, they tend to resolve them after leaving school. They find school or employment where they can excel and not be reminded that they have a disability. Unfortunately, individuals with NLD continue to struggle throughout their lifetime with emotional issues including low self-esteem, anxiety, and depression. In fact, approximately 41% of students diagnosed with NLD are mislabeled by schools as having a severe emotional disability and placed in a classroom for students who do have a severe emotional disability. When this sort of placement happens, one of two things typically happens to students with NLD. They either begin to identify with the aggressive acting out students in an attempt to identify themselves with the aggressor, or they become the target of bullying of the emotionally disturbed student. If the former happens, students with NLD will awkwardly attempts to emulate the aggressor in their classroom, often becoming mascot, henchmen, or yes-man for the bully, or is taken advantage of to perform the illegal acts that the bully would normally perform themselves. If the latter happens (bullying), the student with NLD will again be the target of peers that will further reinforce their perception of the world as unsafe and drive them back to their bedroom where it will be even more difficult in the future to convince them to put themselves out in public and try again.

Individuals with NLD "misperceive, mis-emit, or fail to emit subtle nonverbal information in exchanges with others" (Rourke, 1989). Translated, this means that students who have NLD not only don't understand or pick up on social cues (subtle and not so subtle) that are in their environment, but also do not emit appropriate social cues to others. This is probably one of the most powerful arguments for the need for social skills development throughout the student's school career, not just in elementary school. Social skill development is not intrusive, and no one has ever died from or suffered from social skills that are too well developed. School systems will typically give lip service to their desire to raise good citizens. Being a good citizen demands good socials skills. While most people do not use advanced calculus or trigonometry on a daily basis, all people must use social skills on a continuous basis just to survive in society. While a school can provide a reasonable level of social skills development, those skills must be practiced in a variety of settings to attempt to address the problem of generalization of learned skills. Individuals with NLD can learn most skills or tools to get along in society; however, which tool and when to use it is the greatest struggle that they encounter.

As a result of their need/reliance on auditory input, students with NLD do not need to make eye contact or appear to pay attention. As one student with NLD stated, "Why do I need to look at you when I am getting all the information I need through my ears. I don't need to look at you to hear you." However, in many school settings, by fourth through sixth grades, this type of behavior is often misinterpreted, mislabeled, and test results are misinterpreted as Attention-Deficit Hyperactivity Disorder—Inattentive Type (ADHD–IT). Following this diagnosis, students with NLD are typically placed on a trial of medication to help them pay attention. This tends to be at the very least ineffective, and at the most dangerous as a good portion of students have violent aversive reactions to the medications. By the time these students enter middle school, they have the diagnosis of Anxiety and/or Depression. While behaviorally, these diagnoses correctly describe the student's experience, the emotions remain primarily exogenous to the student. Throughout life, if the environment is recognized as the genesis of the anxiety and altered to be less anxiety producing, a goodly portion of the anxiety and depression dissipates. However, if the student is exposed to an anxiety-producing environment for an extended period of time (different for every individual), a base level of anxiety will become endogenous.

Parents need to create a support system that remains in place over a long period of time. The school, the parents, and the mental health staff need to be collaborating on a regular basis so that a plan is in place when the student with NLD hits the wall emotionally. Much like a three-legged table, if one of these is missing, the supports will fall apart. While the parents may know the child the best, they do not have the educational expertise or the understanding of disorders and interventions that mental health can bring to bear.

A balanced approach must be taken in the relationship between the parents and education officials. While the school cannot be everything to everyone, nor should it be, it does need to step up to the plate with regard to a fully rounded education. Some parents approach the school community with the attitude of "fix my child"; however, a more practical approach would be say, "How are you going to help my son learn what he needs to know to be a happy and productive citizen?" Typically, the school does not have a birth through eighty years old perspective of the parents. They tend to have a Kindergarten through Grade 12 perspective. Whose perspective is correct? Each of them is correct from their perspective. What needs to happen is that they have to develop a new set of goals together as a team. An effective method to do this is by utilizing the McGill Action Planning System (MAPS—refer to Chapter 13) process.

Certainly, the worst-case scenario can be found in the mid to late teenage student that has received little support and who, as a result, is now contemplating suicide. Historically, students with NLD who have gotten to the point of making a decision about killing themselves need immediate intervention. These students have usually done research in the community and on the internet into how to most efficiently kill themselves.

Therapeutically, students need to have had prior contact with a therapist who understands NLD so that they feel comfortable with the therapist when they are truly in need. The therapist will spend some time developing a relationship with the student who can then access the therapist on an as needed basis. This 'as needed' basis can be defined by either the student or the parents. It is also important that the therapist receives weekly feedback from both the school and the parents since adolescents by nature are not forthcoming.

On repeated occasions in life, if the student with NLD is assessed using projective measures (e.g., thematic apperception test, Rorschach, etc.) and/or objective personality measures (e.g., MMPI-A) results may indicate a growing psychotic disorder. The seasoned clinician will look beyond these results and recognize that the disordered thought is a reflection of the NLD and does not portend a psychotic disorder. Again, the clinician must keep in mind that the level of psychosocial disturbance will increase as the lack of support decreases and the complexity of the social situation increases.

Typical Progression of Diagnoses Through the Lifespan for Individuals with NLD

Hearing Impairment

↓

Autism

↓

PDD-NOS

↓

ADHD-Inattentive Type

↓

OCD

↓

Anxiety

↓

Depression

↓

Suicide (Possible)

CHAPTER 8

Implication for Administrators

Developing a Working Relationship with the Student with NLD

The primary role of a building administrator in working with students who have NLD does not vary greatly from that of other students in their building. However, the approach taken in interactions, as well as responsibility to the IEP team, can be quite different. Administrators must continue in their daily functions as guardian of the student progress, educators, curriculum, and facility. For those students identified as Nonverbal Learning Disabled, the building administrator also acts as the translator and guide to this very confusing and dynamic environment.

While the special educator involved will provide the underlying framework of how a school works for the student with NLD, the administrator confirms that there is a system in place. One adult alone cannot and should not alleviate all the fears and anxieties of this student. Other persons of authority need to validate the processes and procedures in place at school. For students with NLD to really believe that a structure is in place and that it is predictable, they will need to have these ideas verified with other members of the school community.

This confirmation of systems and structure occurs through direct instruction. At every interaction, the administrator must remember this student's unusual learning style. Perceptions and understandings that other students may have without question need to be reviewed at the beginning of any conversation. The student with NLD needs to know why he or she is meeting with the administrator, the steps of their conversation, and the possible outcomes of this interaction. It cannot be assumed that they understand why they were called to the office. Whether it is because of a schedule change, a disciplinary issue, or an opportunity to discuss other situations, the administrator needs to be up front with the content and intent of their meeting. It is also helpful to review the role of the administrator with the student at this time.

Using a highly directive stance, will provide more constructive outcomes when working with students with NLD. Often the administrator is asked to play the role of inquisitor, questioning the student in general terms to collect the greatest amount of independent information. This is a very frustrating tact to take with students with NLD. If left with no map to maneuver a conversation, the direction of the interaction will take many twists and turns, and no information will be collected. This will be frustrating for both student and administrator. Providing the expectations and intent of the conversation up front will produce more constructive outcomes.

Balancing the Needs of Student, Parent and School

As a member of the IEP team, the administrator usually assumes the role of the Local Educational Agency or LEA. The primary function of this title is to weigh the needs of the student with the resources of the school. The Individuals with Disabilities Education Act Amendments of 1997 (IDEA) states that the LEA is a member of the educational team who is qualified to provide, or supervise the provision of especially designed instruction to meet the unique needs of children with disabilities. Further, the definition states that the member must be knowledgeable of the school's general curriculum and the resources available of the local educational agency. While in some smaller school systems this may be the special educator, more often this role is held by the building principal who supervises those delivering the service, knows their school's academic program, and is able to release funds so that if necessary additional services can be provided.

While any student may benefit from an IEP, which includes a range of additional resources and services, the job of the administrator is to assist the team in determining which resources and services are needed so that the student can access their education. Though a service may benefit this student, the determining question is need.

Specialized instruction or special education is needed when supports extend beyond what can be provided in the regular classroom or other regular supports. Special education supports can include changes in the curriculum, such as varying the amount of objectives required of the student, adapting the grading system based on the student's current academic levels, and/or teaching daily living skills. Instruction can also be adapted in its delivery to meet the student's learning style, such as augmentative communication, amplification systems or the use of specific behavior plans. In addition, other means of instruction can be provided to be in line with the student's needs.

Federal law provides the framework for determining the special education and related services needs of students with a disability. In determining special education services, the team needs to consider a number of issues. These include looking at the content of the student's classes. Based on what the team knows, does the student need less or more content within their classes to access the concepts presented? Are the instructional approaches used in the classroom appropriate for this child? What classroom practices have worked for this student? How will these changes impact the student's membership in the classroom? While answering these questions, the team also needs to consider how these decisions will help or hinder the student in planning for after high school? How often and to what extent will the specialized instruction occur? Facilitating this discussion not only insures that the students needs are met at the appropriate level, but also that all members of the team are involved in this decision making process.

Once choices are made around specialized instruction, the team may need to consider whether related services are warranted for this child. Related services are defined by IDEA as "transportation, and such developmental, corrective, and other supportive services . . . as may be required to assist a child with a disability to benefit from special education, and include the early identification and assessment of disabling conditions in children." (20 U.S.C. 1400 [Sec. 602] [22]). Related services may include occupational therapy, physical therapy, counseling, a behavioral specialist, or speech/language therapy.

The building administrator assists the team in discussing a number of issues related to the determination of related services. Focusing the process can help take the emotional factor out of the decision making process, so that resources are determined under sound information gathering rather than the desire to overwhelm the student with services or meet parent requests. By clarifying the intent and impact of the service educationally, the team develops its case for the need for such a service.

The team needs to consider how the proposed related service will impact the student's educational program. A related service is needed when the development of the skill or the addressing of an issue can be directly correlated with the student's IEP or success in the classroom. The team should also consider the purpose of the related service. For example, by adding the related service of an occupational therapist, will the result be to assist the team in making decisions about the student's equipment needs, train the staff in making program accommodations and adaptations, and provide the team with technical support? Finally, the team needs to review the educational necessity of the related service. The question is whether the service will allow access and participation in the student's educational program. If the direct line between related service and impact on education is not drawn, then the argument for educational necessity cannot be defended.

The administrator is a key team member in walking the team through this educational decision making process. As the LEA, and purportedly neutral member, the administrator can use this didactic process to allow other team members to present their case for the kinds and extent of services necessary. Allowing the process to work by being prepared to ask the most informative questions is the true intent of the special education process. Coming into the meeting with decisions and a plan all ready in mind creates obstacles to developing trust within the team.

The Administrator's Role on the IEP team

The administrator is not only charged with the responsibility of the LEA, but also needs to serve as the defining vote when the team is at an impasse in making a decision. If consensus is not achieved when making decisions around the student's program, the administrator is put in the position of offering the determining vote. While this seems like a simple answer for a team that is struggling with its choices, it is a last option in the hope to build a constructive IEP team.

The administrator, as one of the facilitators of a strong working team, needs to read the signs of impending conflict and to maneuver the team through these hurdles. Strategies that can help the team include having a clear school vision of the student's needs. The special educator, regular educators, counselor and administrator must be well prepared prior to a full team meeting. This does not mean that decisions are made prior to the IEP meeting, but that the team is prepared with documentation and observations needed prior to the full team meeting. The administrator and special educator can then remind the team in advance of the kinds of questions that will be asked and the evidence necessary to answer those questions. It is also an opportunity to review the special education process and how the system can work. Most importantly, a pre meeting is a time that the team can discuss and clarify the educational needs so that they can be clearly articulated when the family is present. A priority for one educator may be very different from another. If this information is shared ahead of time, the necessary support data can be available. Finally, the pre meeting is an opportunity to develop an agenda for the team meeting that articulates the steps involved in making IEP decisions. Providing a road map for decision-making, allows all team members to know in advance the expected outcomes for the meeting. Parents, as well as educators, need time to process the issues and formulate their responses.

Identification of related services is one opportunity where conflicts may occur (Using the questions above can alleviate some of these potential conflicts.). Another important decision that may cause team stress is deciding on the appropriate environment for this student to receive an education. Federal law mandates that the student receive an education in as close of a setting as possible to their non-disabled peers. The discussion here focuses on how that environment will allow them access to their education. Does the stimulating and dynamic nature in the regular setting provide the right structure for learning that these students need? At the same time, will isolating the student from peers deter his or her social development, which may have later impact on the student's transition out of high school?

Again special education law asks the team to make its decisions based on sound information. In order to determine the right academic setting, observations and related evaluative documentation need to be collected. Based on the student's current successes in the regular education environment, where is the student able to produce academically and where are they adversely affected by their disability? As more supports are put into place, is the student showing greater comfort and achievement? Does the affective testing indicate that the student requires a less anxiety provoking setting? Through a slow process of adding supports and observing student outcomes, the team builds a case for the appropriate learning environment for the student.

While it is important for the administrator to also act as the facilitator and to assist the team in walking through the special education process, the importance of the entire team having the freedom to work together as a whole cannot be understated. The typical questions and their responses become very familiar to those who facilitate IEP team meetings. However, it is important for all team members to explore the possible options for the student through team discussion and debate. Making the team work through the choices develops the necessary commitment to the final program. Though at times it would seem easier to provide the model for the team or a typical response to the questions being asked, each team member brings a different perspective and possible vision of the needs of the student. Individualizing the student program means that the student's specific needs are considered and that the varied options contribute to the final program developed.

In the case when the team is not able to work through the process constructively and consensus is not achieved, it becomes the responsibility of the administrator/LEA to determine the final decision. One strategy in dealing with such an impasse is to defer the decision to a later meeting. By summarizing the differing opinions of the team and allowing team members the time to consider these choices outside of a highly charged conference room, the administrator is providing team members with the time they need to process information. Taking a break also allows for the collection of additional observations and data if needed. Recruiting the expertise of an outside consultant can also be helpful.

On those rare occasions when all the right questions and informative data do not help the team come to consensus, the LEA offers the deciding vote. The parent must then consider whether or not to request the assistance of a mediator to arbitrarily hear the argument or choose to pursue due process. In most decisions, mediation is an option, while with due process it is not. Special education laws, state and federal, define when mediation and due process are possibilities.

Specialized Caseloads

Another role of the building administrator is to consider the various models of special education service delivery. There are many ways to combine the resources of special educators with the needs of students. When making that decision with regards to the specific profile of a student with a nonverbal learning disability, the configuration where special education case managers are assigned students based on a specialization is a model to consider.

Specialized caseloads mean that teachers and students are matched based on a developed skill or expertise that the educator has shown to possess. While the training of special educators allows them to work with a broad range of students with disabilities, each teacher can identify a disability area of greater interest or competency. One special educator may show enhanced skills with cognitively challenged students, while another enjoys working with emotionally disturbed students. By concentrating the efforts of special educators to those students that they have demonstrated underlying strengths, the students benefit from this cultivated expertise. Caseloads that reflect these competencies can enhance the special education program.

The extension of the specialized case manager model is the use of Integration Facilitators as case managers. Again, this designation of case manager allows for the matching of the intensity of student needs with those special educators who have greater experience and well developed skills. The role of the Integration Facilitator is to develop an educational program for students who might not otherwise be able to fully integrate into the regular school environment. These students have more extensive educational needs, may have a broader range of services and service providers, and could include outside consultants to provide technical support to the team. The Integration Facilitator traditionally has a smaller caseload of students in order to assist with the longer list of individual needs. This connection of specialized special educator with students of intensive needs can provide the level of competency needed to work with the significant and varied needs of the student with NLD.

Where students with NLD need support and training both educationally and emotionally, the special educator needs to have training and expertise both in the remediation of specific learning disabilities and in issues of emotional disturbance. The methods and techniques employed to address the student's with NLD learning style are directive and are based on a metacognitive model. Addressing the anxieties related to integrating into a regular school setting must be addressed by someone who understands the nature of anxiety and how it can be managed. Helping the student to negotiate the school environment defines an instructional strategy where educators teach about the thought process employed in the many settings of school. Looking at only one side of this complicated equation will mean that the student is not truly served.

In determining a service model that addresses the needs of the student with NLD, a final consideration for the administrator to consider is that the special educator assigned must have the necessary time and resources to work with this student. The nature of the disability requires that this student have daily interactions with a specially trained educator. They need to verify the student's schedule each day and review the goals and outcomes of their school program. Students with NLD need one-on-one to small group instruction to provide the structure and constant cueing required. They also need a classroom environment that has minimal distractions and a predictable setting. While the needs can be great for the student with NLD, once the properly trained special educator who has access to the time and resources needed for the student's program is in place, this student can thrive and grow in the regular school environment.

Determining the Appropriate Placement

One of the first and most important decisions that the IEP team makes is the identification of an appropriate educational setting for the student. The question is in which school environment will the student be able to access an education? For those students who meet the eligibility criterion for NLD, the range of options can be quite diverse.

The team must always begin its review by first looking at the regular classroom setting. The goal is that the student will be educated with his or her age peers for the greatest amount of time while still meeting educational needs. From this starting point in the traditional classroom, services can then be put in place to support the student's learning style.

Individual programs can vary greatly dependent upon the severity of the student's needs. The majority of students with NLD can be successful educationally with enrollment in regular education classes and support in a special education resource room once daily. Other students with NLD may need the additional support in the classroom of a paraprofessional to assist with the taking of notes, recording and clarification of class assignments, and/or management of a behavior plan. Students with NLD whose emotional needs are primary and who are presenting higher levels of anxiety may need to have portions of their class day in a less stimulating environment than that of the regular classroom. Having opportunities to meet off campus with a tutor or other small group setting may provide the needed break from the intensity of school while maintaining academic progress. There are many variations of these presented models that can adequately address the student's individual needs. The setting is not the sole variable in developing a successful program. Other strategies and approaches applicable to students with NLD must also be in place to be able to assess the appropriate setting for the student.

One of the last educational environments that the team should consider is that of a residential placement. There are occasions when this is the only appropriate educational setting for a specific student as it provides the therapeutic milieu and/or academic specialization that is required by the student's disability. In the case of students with NLD, the consideration of a residential placement must be reviewed with much caution. Students with NLD need their safe place of predictable expectations and personal interactions. Often the only environment that meets this criterion is home and parents. To remove this safety net from these students is extremely concerning. The team must consider the impact of this move, not only on the student's education, but also on their ability to live outside of their comfort zone. The team must weigh the benefit of a therapeutic, highly structured educational environment, against the loss of a daily predictable living setting.

The role of the administrator in working with students with NLD takes on different meanings at different times. Individually, the administrator works to reinforce the structure and systems that have been defined by the special educator. The administrator's intent is clear when meeting directly with the student, and no attempt is made to quiz the student without determining a reference point. They also work to define their role in the school for the student with NLD.

The administrator also serves as the LEA representative. This responsibility dictates that he or she evaluate the educational needs of the student, understand the demands of their school's curriculum, and provide the supervision of special educators that insures that the educational plan is followed. Assessing the needs of the student and weighing these needs with the resources of the school is the primary task of the LEA.

As a key member of the IEP team, the administrator must be cognizant of the kinds of decisions that are to be made and how to negotiate this process. Understanding the questions that need to be asked and how information is collected makes for more effective and less subjective outcomes. Decisions must be made based on clearly observable data that has been collected in a testing setting, through classroom observations, and by reviewing what has worked for the student in the classroom and what has not. Considerations include access to content, beneficial instructional practices, transitional needs for beyond high school, the amount of time needed to deliver the services, and the appropriate educational environment.

As this process unfolds, the administrator takes ownership for the success of the team. Using a defined process that all team members are aware of begins to create a sense of trust among team members. Having coordination meetings in advance of the full team meetings assists with collecting all needed documentation before the questions are asked. These meetings allow school members to be well informed of the student's individual issues and provide time to consider the full array of student needs and resources. These meetings also create an opportunity for an agenda to be drafted. This is shared with parents and outside providers in advance so that they can be adequately prepared for the IEP meeting.

Finally, with regard to the IEP team, the administrator considers the responsibility of providing the defining vote if consensus is not reached. Though this seems to be an easy answer when the team is at an impasse, using the LEA's power to break dissension can critically injure the work of the IEP team. Instead, the administrator's role is to assist the team in continuing to work for the student with interests and needs at the center of the decision making process. The administrator saves the deciding vote for the time when its use is needed to support the child and to allow them to access the right services.

As the building supervisor, the administrator can create an environment of service delivery that can best support the needs of the student with NLD, as well as others receiving IEP services. Various models of special education case management and instructional practices need to be researched to provide the right connection between student need and instructional environment. Specialized caseloads are one system that can provide the appropriate supports for IEP students.

The special educator working with the student with NLD needs a sound background in both the nature of specific learning disabilities and of the issues of students with emotional disabilities. The combination of sound educational practice with the experience of working with students who have significant anxiety disorders allows for the total student to be worked with in the resource room. The use of Integration Facilitators can also provide the quantity of time that is required for appropriate interventions. Administrators must consider the delegation of responsibilities to their special education as they establish the system of service delivery.

Administrators continue to have a long and varied lists of academic "to dos" in their buildings. Meeting the needs of special education students is one facet of their daily operations. While many of the considerations discussed here apply to all students receiving individual education plan services, students with nonverbal learning disabilities can have specific issues which must be addressed in different ways. The relationship that exists between the principal and the student with NLD can feel very directive and authoritarian. The responsibility of the Local Educational Agency (LEA) can take on greater significance as the student's needs are weighed against the school's resources. The role of the administrator on the school team can also be more defined. Finally, establishing a system for service delivery can impact the quality of service provided to the student with NLD and his or her IEP peers. Understanding each of these demands and the tools necessary to negotiate the process is central in effective administration of the educational program for the student with NLD.

CHAPTER 9

Team Development

Identification of Team Leader

Once a child has been diagnosed with NLD, it is imperative that an educational team is developed to specifically meet the educational needs of the child within its respective school. This team could be a 504 team (recognizing the disability with accommodations) or an IEP team. The strength of the team is dictated both by balance and professional respect. The team leader is most often a special educator. There are schools where a guidance counselor or principal is the team leader. It is an exceptional school where the later works well. The team leader is the key to success. They must work hard to be inclusive in their responsibility to spread the word regarding the NLD student and their needs and bring the team to consensus.

Good team building requires a good evaluation and all its components. A history of the student, neuropsychological testing, a speech and language evaluation, educational assessments, physical and occupational therapy assessments if appropriate, a medical exam including vision, and work samples from the classroom are all necessary to build a program. There may be issues of emotional status related to NLD that require a psychologist or psychiatrist is available to support the team and the child. Permission to dialogue with these professionals on an ongoing basis is important to building a working team.

Coordinating the Team

The special educator acts as the conductor and coordinates team information. Key tasks include communicating with the parents to answer questions and concerns and following through on tasks with all teachers and non team members involved with the NLD student. The special educator is the conduit of expertise to assist and support all those involved in the educational process. There are times when it is important to educate the bus driver, athletic coach, and kitchen staff as to good ways to interact with the NLD student. Depending on the age of the student, it is recommended that meetings be held monthly to set a pace for instruction and support. Email or phone communication with the family is very helpful. It is recommended that this be limited to times when questions or events warrant responses. An early, complete scheduling of team meetings is recommended so team members book all meetings to be held and reserve that time for the student. Parent and student schedules should be accommodated when possible. To be efficient, team agendas should be kept to one hour. As you get into the process, there may be team meetings that are not necessary and can be cancelled a month in advance with team approval. If possible, all teachers should attend the monthly meetings. There are school models that rotate the team of teachers to accommodate schedules, but best practice is for all to participate even if it is briefly. Roles should be assigned monthly to all team members: agenda maker, note taker, time keeper, observer. Minutes must be taken to provide a structure of decisions and responsibility for roles. The team must also agree to its process and how it will arrive at decision making. It is a team! The special educator is the team leader with assistance from all other team members, including the parents.

Throughout the school week the team members are communicating on accommodations, assignments, and general well being of the program. It is necessary for accommodations to be well understood by all participants of the team and implemented in the same manner. Many schools have been successful at posting homework and long term assignments on line to assist both students and parents after school hours when misunderstandings most often occur. A daily check of planning books (assignment books) is very helpful for both students and parents. This can be done by the classroom teacher, paraprofessional, or special educator. It is also recommended that a daily specialized study hall be folded into the NLD student schedule so individual or small group instruction in organizational skills, speech and language (social skills training), writing/research projects, modifications and instruction in courses that are more abstract like math and science can be given. Directions need to be broken down into small concrete components for success in accessing class work. This can also be done in class or in the specialized study hall. Left to their own resources NLD students will waste their valuable study time simply because they lack the skills to ask and organize. This study time can make after school more enjoyable if assignments are structured and modified. Work closely with the student on the more challenging assignments at school. Assess those things that can be done with more independence at home, building on success and positive self-image. Fatigue can be a huge factor for the student with NLD. So much more energy is needed to get through a day than is required by non learning disabled students, that homework often becomes a fighting point when they return home at the end of the day. A student with NLD is simply too tired to expend any more energy! This is when things start to fall apart. A team needs to monitor this factor and modify it when necessary.

Curricular Issues

An important component for the team's success is to really understand the strengths and challenges of the curriculum and how the NLD student will interface with that curriculum. The special educator, classroom teacher and paraprofessional assisting in the classroom or with the student must make daily changes/modifications in order to be successful. An example of this shift would be allowing the student with NLD to work with his or her strong verbal skills in place of an art project for a culminating project. A math teacher may use a student's high interest in sports (batting averages) and incorporate that into a curricular unit on averaging numbers in math. It may be helpful for the SLP to attend certain classes to interpret the language and become a strategist for the NLD student in understanding history or English classics. The important thing to remember is that this takes a lot of communication and understanding on all team members' parts to make curriculum accessible to the NLD student.

Assignment completion can be problematic if the team does not agree early on to pace and modify these assignments. Most NLD students cannot organize their time or set themselves up to work. They need structured study areas both at school and home. A double set of textbooks, one for home and one for school, will help eliminate forgetting an important part of homework. They need visual schedules and access to materials that are always in the same locations. An organized binder will be helpful, but still challenging as there are so many things to get together and remember what goes where. Classrooms that are visually stimulating can be a sensory overload issue for the NLD student. Most NLD students can barely maneuver down the hall and find their class, let alone go through a maze of desks that have different colored name tags. They will learn all these skills if given the verbal information, instruction and assistance. The team has to make it all happen.

Grading and assessments can be designed by the team in small group working sessions or generally conceived at the team meetings. It is important that all agree that the NLD student will be assessed individually part of the time. Individual discussion sessions with the instructors to explain and exhibit their understanding of the course information are very helpful. This would be in lieu of a written exam. Written exams can be designed by the special educator and teacher to access the student's strengths through structure of choices and written requirements. Group projects are challenging as the social component is always present. The student with NLD can work in groups if the group dynamics are set up ahead of time to cater to his or her strengths. Grading criteria needs to be interpreted and the method agreed upon by the team as it should be different for the student with NLD so he or she is not penalized because of a disability.

The team concept works exceedingly well for the NLD student when planned and organized by a group of professional educators working with parents and other service providers. There is a lot of organization that must take place and constant communication regarding modifications and accommodations. The important factor is to constantly revise and revise to benefit the student. NLD students have the same learning capacity, they simply have to take a different tact to reach their goal. The rewards that come to the school team are amazing, but more amazing is what the NLD student is able to learn and synthesize.

CHAPTER 10

Integrating the Student with NLD
Into the Regular Classroom

The Regular Educator's Role in Working with the Student with NLD

Each member of the educational team has a unique relationship with the child who has a nonverbal learning disability. The classroom teacher spends the greatest amount of school time with this student and therefore needs to have a firm understanding of their unique traits. The ideal situation is to have one teacher with a small group of students each day who have similar learning characteristics. Instead, class lists can exceed a hundred students each day bringing a broad range of academic styles to the classroom. The regular educator needs to have training so as to be prepared to welcome the student with NLD into the classroom amongst all the other students.

Teachers must first know that these students bring their own dynamic to their classroom. The majority of these students have academic capabilities that exceed the average student. Their strong language skills can allow them to contribute constructively to classroom discussions and to explore their ideas creatively in written form. Most students with NLD are highly motivated to be a productive member of a class. They also bring their own sense of humor and quirkiness that can be refreshing for the teacher. Once these students feel welcomed and at ease in a classroom, they are a positive addition to any class.

One of the first advantages of having a student with NLD in the regular classroom is that a great deal of information has been collected regarding this student. Whether the student has a specific educational plan or not, it is probable that either an educational team has met regarding this student's needs and has requested a comprehensive evaluation to address learning concerns or that the student's parents have pursued this testing to better understand their child. In either situation, the regular educator is able to gleam a better understanding of this student's strengths to the classroom as well as possible challenges.

If the student has not met the eligibility guidelines for special education services or 504 protection, this would indicate that the student has managed to develop strategies to be successful in the regular setting. The testing data is still available for the teacher to review, though specific accommodations are not warranted. In the case that an IEP or 504 plan is in place, the teacher is then given a brief description of the student's learning style, a specific set of instructions for working with this student in the classroom, and a list of yearly goals. While the quantity of information about one child may be overwhelming, the regular educator is also provided with a range of supports, including a special educator or a 504 coordinator to work with the classroom teacher and a team of educators that works to support the student in being successful through out the school.

Included in the student with NLD's education plan is a list of educational practices that will assist the student in accessing the material presented in the classroom. Many of the strategies that are most advantageous in working with students with NLD are also best practices in instruction for all students. These include a highly structured classroom environment that provides a predictable format for the daily schedule, work submissions, homework assignment communication, and behavioral expectations. Further, those teachers who provide weekly planners that document the academic goals and expectations for the week are incredibly helpful. Every student benefits from those systems that clearly communicate the teacher's goals and expectations and provide predictability in the classroom.

Students with NLD bring to the classroom strong language abilities. The more opportunities that they have to engage with the material verbally, the better able they will be to understand the concepts presented. In fact, if the idea to be learned is first discussed with the class and then presented visually, the student with NLD will have a point of reference when the visual representation is displayed. At times, it may even be important that the student with NLD is cued not to engage with the visual material and is instead asked to attend to the discussion around the chart, graph or other visual representation. This will allow him or her to access their stronger learning style.

Other classroom strategies to consider include the use of models to better define the end product. When first presented with a long-term project, the student with NLD begins to explore a vast array of options. The classroom teacher can assist with the successful completion of this assignment by stating at the onset what they wish the student would achieve. Providing sample reports, previously completed posters, or other written end products gives the student with NLD a view of the final goal. When they begin the assignment, they will know in which direction to go. For some students with NLD, they may even need to have the choice of topic or project limited to only one or two options. Too many decisions can be overwhelming for these students.

When planning assignments, the teacher needs to consider the strengths and challenges of the student with NLD. They are verbal learners and can therefore best communicate their competencies with the material in a verbal format. As the teacher lists the variety of means that a project can be presented, be certain that a spoken report is a choice available to them. This may mean, however, that the student presentation will be given to a smaller group or to the teacher solely if the individual education plan calls for this accommodation.

If the purpose of the project is to provide a visual representation of an idea, the teacher should consider a variety of ways that a poster or other manipulative can be constructed. The use of computer generated photographs or recreations of artwork can be one way that the student with NLD can participate. Also, Power Point presentations constructed with the assistance of a teacher allows the student with NLD to list ideas in a format that can be shared with others. The special education teacher may be asked to provide a more detailed model, chart or graphic representation that the student can then recreate in a visual format. The creation of maps or coloring in of key points on a map will also require direct instruction by the special educator. Visual representation of ideas provides an important avenue to assist with learning of other students, while it creates dilemmas for the child with NLD.

Classroom behavior management is another important consideration. Predictability again comes into play with clear consistent expectations. The classroom teacher needs to look for other symptoms of school anxiety in the class. This may appear as extended trips to the nurse or bathroom. Conversations that avoid the task rather than engaging with the work presented and other behaviors that demonstrate that the student is not intellectually engaged are important to consider. In those situations, cueing the student to the task and offering reminders regarding the structure can get him or her back on track.

Once the individual learning style of the student with NLD is considered, integration into the regular curriculum can be constructive and less of an obstacle. Knowing that the structure and predictability of the classroom is in place is the first element of classroom management that the student with NLD requires. Also, having a clear picture of the teacher's expectations, both academically and behaviorally, provides additional stability. Further, accessing the student's superior verbal abilities allows the teacher to have a more accurate view of the material mastered. Providing accommodations around more visual tasks means that this learning challenge is not an obstacle to student success.

Accommodations Versus Modifications

Two important integration terms, accommodations and modifications, need to be understood by the classroom teacher. Accommodations are the adaptations of curriculum and class environment that allow special needs students to access the regular classroom. In contrast, modifications are significant changes to the content that allow the ideas to be accessible to the student. For the student with NLD, accommodations are the more often used special education tool for integration into the regular classroom.

Accommodations are the kinds of adaptations that can be made that allow for a student's learning style to be considered beyond traditional methods of educational practice. They may include extended time for assignments, modifications to the kind and quantity of reinforcement problems that are required of the student, or how a presentation is given in the classroom. The decisions as to which accommodations are given are based on evaluative and observational data and are made during the development of the student's program. The student's IEP outlines and defines the kinds of accommodations the student mst receive in order to access an education. By the time that a classroom teacher sees the student's IEP and list of accommodations, they are non-negotiable and they can only be changed or adapted through the IEP process.

In contrast, modifications imply that the student will need significant changes to the content of the course in order to access the concepts. This may mean that the classroom teacher is asked to identify the primary concepts that are relevant to the coursework and that these ideas are developed in conjunction with the special educator. Students receiving a modified program usually continue to attend the regular class. They may, however, not be there for the full length of time and could return to the resource room for direct instruction in some concepts. The use of modifications for a student program means that the student's learning needs are severe enough to warrant a major change to the program being offered to all other students. Again, the decision to use program modifications is made through the IEP team and is based on existing data and observations.

The use of accommodations and modifications is to insure that the student's learning style is considered when accessing the least restrictive environment. These are the guidelines that the IEP team has determined that a classroom teacher needs to be aware of and accountable to do so that the student can access the regular classroom. Some accommodations are general, such as cueing the student to attend when they may appear to be unfocused. Other accommodations may be more specific such as the use of specific strategies when assessing a student's understanding of concepts. Modifications are a less often-used special education practice that is only in place for students with significant learning needs.

Accommodations that Address the NLD Learning Style

A range of accommodations may be needed to incorporate the particular learning style of the student with NLD. The development of accommodations by the IEP team is based on a thorough review of the testing and observational data collected, as well as by what is known of the nature of the student with NLD. While there are many possible accommodations, each should be considered for its merits, but not all should be included. Accommodations, like academic and emotional goals, are individualized.

One important area, when considering possible accommodations, is assessment. For the student with NLD a number of issues impact the ability to be fairly assessed. First, the learning style implies that longer essay test formats may cause much confusion for the student as attempt are made to determine the intent of the question. Time is then consumed by making decisions about what the teacher is asking and what the response should be. Instead, short answer format, true/false questions, or fill-in-the-blank allow these students to have a clearer understanding of the concepts the teacher is assessing. In addition, the construction of the test needs to be considered. The student with NLD can be quickly visually overloaded. Thus, an assessment that has increased space with questions spread over additional pages will be less confusing. If visual representations are used, such as maps, graphs or geometric representations, color may need to be added to their individual test for better understanding.

Another important consideration for the student with NLD and assessment is the atmosphere of the classroom when taking the test. Anxiety is always a consideration when program planning for these students. This is especially true for assessment. Whether it is the sound of other students turning the pages of their test or the uncertainty of what the teacher is asking, providing a quiet, less distracting environment for assessment is important. The additional time needed to clarify test questions must also be considered. Further, the student with NLD needs to make this nonverbal task, verbal. That is to say that permission needs to be given to read the test questions aloud so verbal strengths can be accessed by the student. It is not that they are engaging with a teacher in conversation, but they are simply using the verbal modality to clarify for themselves what is being asked of them and to develop a response that is appropriate and accurate. The student may, in addition, need to follow up the written portion of the assessment with a dialogue with the teacher to ensure that a clear response has been given.

Curriculum issues must also be considered when providing accommodations in line with this learning style. Independent reading is a visual task, and for some students with NLD it needs to be accessed auditorily. This allows for comprehension to be at a level commensurate with the student's true ability. Use of tape-recorded books or technology that allows for documents to be scanned and read back provides this access. Further, the quantity of material reviewed and produced may need to be considered. The types of accommodations and specialized instruction needed to access the concepts may dictate a decrease on the number of academic requirements placed on the student with NLD. Consultation with the special educator as to the extent of these accommodations is critical so that the expectations are equitable to the student's abilities.

How the student with NLD locates information, whether through the school library or computer, is important to determine. Locating the classroom can be difficult enough, but to ask him or her to identify multiple sources to support a thesis is extremely challenging. The library requires that each student is able to use a variety of sources to find materials or that they access the librarian for assistance. This can be mission impossible. Using the computer to access information also requires too many choices. In this situation, the accommodation could range from providing the student with the sources needed to complete the task, to giving detailed directions as to how to independently locate the information.

The emotional needs of the student with NLD can also impact the kinds of accommodations that are made available to this student. At the start of the school year, as these students begin to assimilate their new schedule, teachers, and peer groups, their anxiety can be one of their greatest obstacles to learning. These students may need easy access to a less stimulating environment, such as the resource room or counseling office without question or confrontation. A behavior plan can be developed that establishes a clear process as to how to intervene with a student when signs of anxiety are obvious. This plan could include scripted responses to student behavior or an established routine that includes simple cueing so that the student can assess strategies for reducing stress.

Other kinds of accommodations can be considered that allow access. These may include how students communicate their understanding of the material. When asked to present their ideas to the class, they may instead select a smaller group to share their information with so that the anxiety is decreased. The student with NLD may also require weekly written progress reports from the teacher to confirm an accurate understanding of his or her progress in the class since the student's perception of their status in a class can be extremely off target.

Accommodations allow the student to access an education in an environment as close to the regular setting as possible. Significant changes to the content and structure of the course are not required. Instead, the teacher is asked to consider a variety of adaptations to instruction methods, curriculum, class environment, and assessments. Once understood and in place, the student can successfully function in this setting, and the classroom teacher can begin to enjoy the many strengths and qualities that this student can bring to the classroom.

The Homework Issue

The issue of homework is one characteristic of the student with nonverbal learning disabilities that must be considered. While this is most often addressed through special education services, the classroom teacher needs to be aware of the issues surrounding homework completion for the student with NLD. Work completion and production in general can be extremely challenging for these students. Their verbal skills are superior to their ability to produce. While they are able to articulate a detailed understanding of the material and can usually extend the understanding beyond the current concept, the translation of these verbal ideas into a written product is extremely difficult and frustrating for the child with NLD.

The approach of the special educator is to determine which academic work they are able to complete independently and which needs specialized assistance. In addition, the time needed to complete this work must be considered. Thus, homework quantity must be reviewed. The end product may also be accommodated to assist with work completion.

Homework for students with NLD needs to be addressed at school as much as possible. Homework at home can become a nemesis. The student with NLD will sit at a table for hours with books and paper before them and get nothing accomplished. Difficulties with understanding the intent of an assignment, tangential thought, and initiation of tasks are significant obstacles in completing this work. The frustration level quickly increases as parents try to illicit information from their child that just isn't there. Using the resource room as the primary site for homework completion produces much stronger results. In this specialized environment, assignments are clarified for intent, goals are established to complete tasks, and immediate feedback is available to verify accuracy and quality.

Using the special educator as a conduit for work completion may mean that more time is spent in the resource room and less coursework time is available. While intellectually these students can engage with a large quantity of concepts, mastering these ideas through reinforcement activities can become overwhelming. Having the access to the special educator to insure that the course work is thoroughly understood and to allow the student to achieve at a level commensurate with their ability is significant. Overloading the student with classes is extremely frustrating and not rewarding for either the student or the teacher.

Once in the resource room, the special educator begins by reviewing the intent of the assignment, using teacher provided models to discuss with the student the end product, and identifying the steps involved to complete the assignment. In addition, the special education teacher and student discuss how the project will be completed, outline dead lines for the steps in an assignment book, and monitor the completion of each task. This metacognitive process allows the student with NLD to look at learning externally and to see that it is a well-sequenced process. This is extremely challenging for these learners who need this detailed modeling to begin to understand the steps involved in work completion.

Considering the process involved with homework completion, it is understandable why the largest quantity of homework needs to be initially completed in school. Another characteristic of the student with NLD is that once outside of the school environment these students need to regroup emotionally after a day of intense social demands. Most often, these are students who need to go home at the end of the day and have time alone or time to find those activities that do not create the social demands of school and allow time to regroup personally. For some, it is re-reading a comforting book, playing a video game or watching a movie. It is a time for them to step back and observe rather than engage. As a result of this behavior and need, the student with NLD has even less time to address homework.

Considering both the learning and emotional needs of these students is important when determining the quantity of homework and location for completing assignments. An important accommodation to consider as an IEP team is how much and where homework is completed. Each student is different; however, the student's cognitive ability cannot be the sole determinant when making this decision.

Communication Between Home and School

As the regular educator understands the individualized needs of the student with NLD, communication between teacher and special educator is imperative. In addition, the contact with home and parents is equally important. Parents and students need consistent feedback about how the student is performing, how they are integrating into the classroom, and what additional systems may be put into place. This information needs to come not only from the special educator but also from the view of the regular educator. Systems for communication can include weekly progress notes, emails, and short phone calls. The child with NLD may have such an inaccurate view of their successes and challenges in the regular environment that this verification of progress is critical.

In contrast, there is a time when the sharing of information becomes too much. The student with NLD should not feel that he or she is living under a microscope and that every move will be scrutinized. Quick, clear comments that inform but that do not assign blame are helpful. Belabored evaluation of systems and their value can be detrimental. Parents need to be in the know about student progress, but students should not feel that they are constantly being re-evaluated. This does not create a sense of confidence and competence for the student.

The inclusion of any student into a classroom dictates that the teacher is aware of the learning style and academic capabilities of that child. The expectation of teachers is that they have that awareness for all of their students. When a student with NLD walks through the door, he or she comes with a plan in hand that outlines individual strengths, challenges, goals and accommodations. The teacher does not have to spend a great deal of time determining needs, as might be necessary to do with other children, instead just incorporating this plan into the daily instructional practices.

This first consideration for the teacher is how the inclusion of this student with NLD impacts how the classroom is run. The idea of a structured classroom with a set routine, the use of weekly planners, the incorporation of multiple modalities in instruction, the presentation of models to view the end product, and clear expectations for behavior with set responses, are all sound educational practices that most students can benefit from academically. None of these ideas are novel classroom strategies and can become an additional tool that a teacher can incorporate into daily practice. The student with NLD is not requiring extreme revisions of the teacher's usual script.

The student's with NLD Individual Education Plan clearly outlines the kinds of accommodations and/or program modifications that the student needs in order to access an education. In most cases, the IEP will identify the kinds of adaptations to presentation, curriculum, and assessment that the individual student needs. While many accommodations can be considered, not all are required. As the IEP team better understands the student's specific needs, it can narrow down those accommodations that are significant for the individual student's learning style. Again for most students with NLD, this list can include subtle changes to presentation and instruction that can become part of the daily routine. More significant adaptations can occur with the assistance of the special educator, such as how to accommodate a test, assessment or long-term project.

Homework is one important classroom practice that needs to be understood by the classroom teacher. Often the student with NLD is first identified as having an academic issue when his or her verbal output in class does not match his or her written production. Along with their social quirks, these students can bring much to the classroom when they participate in class discussions yet seem unable to start any task when left on their own. The amount of intervention needed to translate the teacher expectation into a student driven end product is immense. As a result of this issue, homework is often begun in class, further clarified in the special education resource room, and finalized at home. The intensity of this behavior can mandate that a decrease in the quantity assigned, not quality, is considered. These students often desire to produce at a level commensurate with their classmates; however, their learning style dictates that this is not possible.

Home and school communication is often the role of the special educator for students with individual education plan. In the case of students with NLD, the voice of the classroom teacher is extremely valuable in giving another perspective to the classroom experience. Though their every movement should not be scrutinized, the ability to obtain an accurate perception of how instruction and assessment are progressing is important information that the parent needs to receive.

The relationship of the regular educator and student with NLD is very important to the student. As he or she looks for confirmation of their abilities, what occurs in the regular classroom becomes a measure of potential for future success. When the teacher gains an understanding of this student, they are able to see many strengths and wonderful qualities that are brought into the classroom. Discovering the unmet potential of this young person is often what the regular education teacher takes from the experience of having a student with NLD in the classroom.

CHAPTER 11

Intervention Strategies and Specialized Instruction

Determining the Right Approach and Intervention

Once roles are defined and relationships are developed, the special educator applies his or her craft as an educator. Finding the right approaches and modes of intervention to allow the student with NLD to achieve academically and emotionally becomes the primary focus of the special educator. What is accomplished in the resource room as the result of appropriate specialized instruction is nothing short of magic. When the student is finally able to access the intellect that he or she possesses verbally and apply this ability to other modes of production, the student feels a potential is beginning to be realized and the educators, who knew the possibility for success was there, can see it happen.

Having the right list of strategies and instructional interventions is the key to working this magic. The learning style of the student with NLD dictates a very different intervention mode than is used for other students with disabilities. At times, it may appear dictatorial and overbearing, while at other times the special educator can feel more engaged with the student. Once the processes are in place and the student is comfortable with these new systems for learning, the student/teacher relationship can feel more normalized.

The approaches used with the student with NLD address his or her specific learning style. Structure is the underlying theme.

This not only applies to the resource room environment but also the strategies used to address the production of work and the assimilation of new ideas. The ideas and concepts that these students possess need to find a route that will allow this information to be communicated to others. They also need to understand the underlying processes that will allow them to master the material presented. The special educator can never assume that the student with NLD has the correct perception of how to complete a task. All that may have seemed obvious to other students in the past needs to be reviewed, discussed, and taught to the student with NLD. When the thoughts are unlocked, the student can demonstrate the broad range of competencies held.

Written Language

The ability to verbalize ideas is the primary strength for the student with NLD. Strong vocabulary skills, making connections between ideas, and ability to communicate the content that is being presented to them is evident. The difficulty occurs when the student is asked to translate these verbal ideas into a written product. One of two situations often occurs. Either the student feels overwhelmed by the ideas circulating in his or her head and cannot even begin the task, or they start immediately and are left with a jumble of ideas that have little continuity. The result is a heap of tangential thoughts with no structure. The goal of the special educator is to help the student translate ideas into a form that others can appreciate and understand.

How thoughts are constructed and/or communicated is the first issue to address. The purpose for requiring a written product is usually to have some mode to assess the student's understanding of the material presented and to see their ability to make connections between new ideas and what has been previously learned. The first question then becomes, for assessment purposes, does the student need to demonstrate this competency in a written format? Can the student tape record his or her ideas and present the tapes to the teacher? Can the student outline his or her ideas through a computer presentation and give a verbal report to the class, the teacher, or a small subset of students and teacher? If the goal of the assessment is to demonstrate an understanding of content and to expand that awareness, than selecting the appropriate format for that presentation is important. The student's knowledge of the material is what is important. The difficulties with written language should not be assessed at this time.

The student with NLD, however, cannot avoid the need to put ideas into a written format. It would be a significant loss for the student if he or she were not able to develop a strategy to convey their extensive ideas into a product that can be shared with others. The role of the special educator at this point is to put a structure in place for the child so that he or she can see that written discourse can closely parallel verbal thought. The student needs to see that the point from thought to paper is short and that translating these ideas to paper is not a labored process.

The special educator needs to recognize first that the ideas circulating in the student's mind are of a high quality with sophisticated vocabulary, varied sentence structure and connected experiences. The difficulty is the randomness of these thoughts. Applying a structure to the mental conversation is the first step. In order to begin to sequence verbal ideas to a written output, the student with NLD needs to understand the structure of the final product.

The intervention strategy for written language begins by verbalizing and outlining what the final product will look like. Demystifying the writing process is critical to the successful remediation of this skill. The special educator begins by teaching the components of a sentence, a paragraph and then an essay. This could be as singular as asking what are the parts of a good sentence? The sentence begins with a noun that is acted upon by a strong verb which is further enhanced by supporting details. Sharing good sentences from a current text, both by discussion and dissection on the board, gives the student with NLD an understanding of the blueprints for building a good sentence. The student is then allowed to produce examples verbally of good sentences while the special educator writes them down. For the student, this demonstrates that he or she possesss the capabilities to build a good sentence. Relating these skills to a current assignment completes the bridge from isolated task to the practicality of daily class work.

The next step in the student's development as writers is to apply this dissective process to the paragraph format. Again the special educator teaches the components of a strong quality paragraph. Examples from current content work show the student the end product that the teacher is looking for when they assess for competency. At times, using a math-like algorithm, a topic sentence + specific supporting details + a concluding sentence = a paragraph, gives the student with NLD the teacher's expectations upfront.

Often a stumbling block is that the student does not know the world's expectations. The clearer that educators can be about what they want from their students with NLD, the more successful the students can become. Having a paragraph algorithm in their minds, allows for a greater probability of success at a level commensurate with their ability.

Finally, at the essay level, the student and teacher begin with the same process. Reflecting on quality essays that are at the student's current reading comprehension level allows the student to see the end product. Breaking the essay into its primary components is the next step. This is done both with production and, at times, with a visual representation. The visual map can be done with a series of blocks of various sizes. The page may have a large box on top representing the introductory paragraph, followed by three smaller boxes to show the supporting detail paragraphs, and end with a last box of a larger size to indicate the concluding paragraph.

When constructing the paragraph verbally, it may be helpful to begin with the thesis idea and then move directly to the supporting details. Once the details are fleshed out and the special educator has recorded these ideas in the boxes provided, the student can then see how the introductory paragraph contains notations of the details and that the concluding paragraph summarizes those thoughts. Building the puzzle of an essay and using this process until the steps are internalized, demonstrates to the student with NLD the process that good writers use and that he or she may not understand.

The intent of this activity is to allow the student with NLD to understand the structure first so that following this structure a response can be formulated mentally. When the student is expected to formulate ideas, output these thoughts and then fit them into a structured response, there are too many expectations. Allowing the student to compose within his or her mind and then to produce in written form is more constructive and requires fewer external steps.

As the student with NLD progresses to longer essay formats, such a structured format as described above is usually not needed. Instead, the special educator and student verbalize this process, possibly using the boxed sheet as a cueing system. The special educator should record the verbal brainstorm, placing the ideas in a sequence that makes sense. Questions are asked by the teacher to sustain the idea and to ensure that the topic stays within the thesis of the paper. At this point of the student's development as a writer, the role of the special educator is to cue the questions that will eventually be internalized by the student. The teacher models the thought process verbally that is used by most writers.

While some of the systems discussed may be faded out, the need to discuss the content of the paper by thoroughly mapping out the process for completing the assignment, insuring that the student understands the intent of the assignment, and verbally brainstorming the student's ideas around the thesis, may continue to be needed as an external support. The goal of this developmental strategy is to articulate the processes of thought that are needed to write. This metacognitive process, thinking about thinking, is the critical step in understanding the nature of intervention for the student with NLD.

Reading Comprehension

While students with NLD are notorious reading decoders, the depth of their understanding of what they read can vary greatly. The issue here is the student's ability to understand the inner workings of personal interactions in narrative writing as well as his or her ability to identify what is important in contextual tasks. Fiction writing, where characters interact, can be very confusing for the student with NLD. Understanding personal interactions that play out in front of them is confusing enough. Extracting meaning from interactions that occur in text is even more difficult. Nonfiction writing, where fact upon fact is presented, can overwhelm the NLD student as they weigh what is the key concept and what are supporting details. If a number of photographs or charts are thrown in to support the material, such as in a history or math text, they can become visually distracted.

As is true of the other approaches presented thus far, the first step in both fiction and nonfiction comprehension, is to break down the task of understanding written material to the most basic elements. Again the student with NLD needs to see the underlying steps that, when put together, allows an individual to understand what has been read.

In narrative writing, this process begins at the short essay level. The student is presented with a short narrative piece and is given a verbal map of its content. The special educator outlines the format of a good piece of writing; this includes how characters are introduced, the intent of the first few paragraphs, and how conflict is introduced, builds overtime, and is finally resolved.

Prior to reading the piece, the student is given some questions to ask him or herself while reading. These questions include: Can they make a personal connection to an event or situation?, Where are the characters introduced?, Do they see the conflict presented?, What events cause the conflict to build?, How does the conflict become resolved?, and Where are they personally confused by in the piece? As they read, the student is asked to make a notation with a small sticky note. After completing the reading, the teacher then goes back with the student to review and respond to the notes.

The first time this intervention is presented, the student is asked aloud so that the note system can be modeled. Each question needs to be discussed thoroughly to insure understanding of the intent of the question. Making personal connections is especially difficult for the student with NLD. Specific examples may need to be highlighted, and the student is then asked to explore in their own life experiences how this can be related. This is a difficult conversation at times, but a meaningful one. The student with NLD needs the opportunity to work through personal interactions verbally so that the teacher can redirect misperceptions. How and why characters interact is a key component (and a significant stumbling block) in the understanding of written material for these students.

Once the student is able to internalize the questions and understand the steps, he or she can then read silently and then discuss the piece of work with the special educator. The use of sticky notes may be phased out, and the student may begin to make written notes in the margins of text or record ideas on a separate sheet of paper. It is helpful for the student to record thoughts while reading in order to focus their discussion later with the teacher or to organize a later written summary. Often, if asked to read through a piece without taking stock of what is happening, the student is overwhelmed with all of the information at the end of piece and has lost the overall purpose of the writing. Taking notes in one form or other is very helpful in avoiding this issue.

The goal of this strategy is to again understand the underlying process involved in comprehending narrative writing. The special educator can not assume the student with NLD knows the steps that a good reader uses to negotiate a piece of writing. The steps involved must first be externalized, then reviewed and practiced before the student can use them without assistance. As the steps become part of the student's repertoire of skills, less teacher support is needed.

The development of comprehension for nonfiction material follows a similar format. A piece of content based material is presented from a current academic course. The special educator verbally defines and describes the typical format of a nonfiction paragraph. The student must know that a paragraph usually begins with a topic sentence, supporting details follow and a concluding sentence summarizes the main idea of the paragraph.

The student and special educator practice dissecting paragraphs, answering the following questions. How does the topic sentence focus the paragraph? Are supporting details used to support the main idea? Does the final sentence restate the main idea? Subsequent paragraphs are presented where the topic sentence may be imbedded later in the paragraph, where extraneous details are presented and evaluated for their support of the main idea, and where a concluding sentence may not exist. It is important to start with a paragraph that follows the originally stated format before later paragraphs with varied formats are presented. The student with NLD needs practice cracking the code of a paragraph so that the format is understood and not assumed.

From the simple paragraph format, the special educator then presents longer pieces of text. It is important to discuss with the student with NLD the use of section headings to define the content. One often used strategy is to begin each piece of content based material by taking each heading, bold faced or italic word, and captions beneath pictures, and then creating questions from each of these cue words. Verbally walking the student with NLD through a section in a text book and showing him or her how these textual cues define the main ideas of a piece is important so that the student is aware of this structure while reading. This code is again not obvious to the student with NLD; however, once the strategy is learned and the student feels confident that it works, it is an approach that he or she will usually apply when reading.

An additional use of this strategy of forming questions from cue words is as an approach for reviewing content material for teacher assessments. Rather than having the student review notes by visually scanning content, using the question based verbal review of material not only substantiates the importance of this strategy, but is more aligned with the student's learning style. Relying on their verbal strengths to access their understanding of material is the appropriate way to prepare for assessments.

While the students with NLD are known for their strong verbal skills, acquiring new vocabulary in an area that the student does not have a great deal of experience with can be challenging. Relying on their verbal strengths can be the most direct route in developing a strategy for developing this skill. Discussing with the student the list of key concepts, attending to the highlighted words in the text, and previewing content by determining what is all ready known about the subject assists the student in developing a working knowledge of the material. Specific vocabulary can be addressed by determining the key elements to the meaning of a word or term. Questions used to limit the content of the definition include: Does this word relate to the key concept?, How does the term differ from other vocabulary presented?, and What parts of the definition are most critical in understanding the term?

Once the words or terms are reduced to their key components verbally, they can be rewritten by the student containing this new code. They are then reviewed aloud as often as possible and in a variety of settings. When presented with these words in an assessment task, the ability to read the test aloud is significant to cue this mode of understanding. Assessments can always be accommodated to include a word bank, to group words according to overlying themes, to spread the content over a number of pages rather than reduced to one page with limited white space, or to be given verbally by the teacher. With these accommodations, the assessment will more accurately determine the student's working knowledge of the material. This dialogue regarding vocabulary should be used whenever new words are presented. Using other visual systems to develop understanding is not the most advantageous and can confuse the student in mastering the material.

Reading comprehension as is seen in the development of other academic competencies, needs to rely on the student's with NLD strengths. When this is forgotten, the student uses inefficient modes of collecting, storing and retrieving new ideas. Not only does the special educator need to employ these strategies, but must also educate the student with NLD how these systems work. The special educator's job is both to get the information in and out, and also give the student an understanding of how his or her brain works and how to become an independent learner.

Mathematics

Of all the academic areas, mathematics can be the most challenging for the student with NLD. Math relies on the visual mode to communicate a large quantity of ideas in a limited amount of space. Trying to incorporate verbal strengths in this visual process is the goal of instruction and remediation in this area. The more the task can be made into a verbal process, the greater the chance that the student with NLD will incorporate the ideas.

Mathematic's reliance on visual cues needs to be translated for the student with NLD. Often a variety of applications will be required of the student in a mathematical task. The student is asked to use visual information to determine which system or procedure to use. The special educator with the NLD student needs to crack this visual code verbally. This entails the student's and teacher's outlining the steps required to complete the mathematical process. A script for completing a specific mathematical procedure is then created.

It is helpful for the teacher to scribe this script into a notebook where all mathematical scripts are kept. The notebook is set up in a two column format with the student's identified steps in one column and an example of this kind of problem in the second column. Having the steps in line with the example for reference and review simplifies how the information is stored and retrieved by the student. While visual cues are presented with the example problem, the script is readily available for understanding. This notebook can later be used as a test accommodation to be available to the student during assessments if determined by the IEP team.

When deciding which materials or texts will be used for math, choose those resources that develop the awareness of the concept prior to introducing the algorithm. A greater focus on language is used for these programs, allowing the student with NLD to verbally understand the idea before being presented with the system of how to complete the problem. The more language that is available to understand the underlying principals of an idea, the greater the probability of understanding for this student.

Textbooks, however, which provide a large number of visual stimuli that is extraneous to the development of a specific idea can be overwhelming for these students. The student with NLD has difficulty separating what is significant and what is not. A selection of resources and texts that can enhance the understanding of students with NLD and take advantage of their cognitive strengths is critical in the development of their mathematical skills.

Once materials are identified and the process is reduced to a set script, the student with NLD must develop a routine for completing written work. Discussing with the student how a paper should be set up and what the teacher expects is important to correct any misperceptions. Having a script notebook on hand ensures that the student applies the procedure consistently. Cueing the student to spread work across the page rather than being limited to one sheet of paper gives him or her the visual space to understand the concept. This process may be modeled at the board with a problem set given for homework and is then scribed by the student into a notebook. Eventually, once the student has incorporated this process, effort should be made to complete the work in the notebook without the board reinforcement.

As the student completes the work the special educator should check it for accuracy. If any misperceptions as to how to complete the assignment are evident, these should be corrected as the student with NLD will not usually check their work after every problem has been completed. This can lead to the same error being made throughout the work. The student with NLD will respond well to constant and consistent reinforcement, and often may not be aware of an incorrect algorithm. For purposes of homework, the special educator may ask the student to complete three or four of the more difficult problems under the teacher's supervision so that the student can demonstrate an understanding. The homework then becomes the remaining less challenging problems. This not only develops the student's competency with the concept, but also allows the student to develop additional confidence in this area.

No matter what the mathematical concept, the intent of specialized instruction for mathematics is to take ideas that have been formed visually into the verbal realm. Acting as the translator and allowing the student to put words to their understanding takes the mystery out of mathematics. Math instruction relies heavily on visual modeling. The special educator must find other means to develop the same ideas, but without the focus on the student's eyes.

Study Skills

The thread that holds all of the course work together is how the student brings his or her ideas together in an organized framework. The special educator can not trust that the student with NLD will independently develop a system of organization that has the level of structure that is needed. Just as verbal thoughts are organized cognitively before they go from pen to paper; materials need to have a set location for storing and a system for retrieval. Once in place, the student has the confidence of knowing how to record information in class, store materials collected in class, set academic priorities once in the resource room, and keep completed work for class submission.

The first step in this process for the special educator is to assess what systems are currently in place (if there are any) and what parts of the existing system are working for the student. There are many study skills systems that have varying degrees of external structure, and it is important to choose a system that the student will agree to and take advantage of in the classroom. Having one set method that all students will comply with is unrealistic. The development of a study skills approach needs to occur with the student involved so that he or she has greater ownership.

When the backpack is opened, it is important to take inventory of its contents. Does the student prefer one kind of notebook over another? It may not be important why they selected a specific style of notebook, as much as that they have all ready attempted to set up a system. This should not be dismissed. If there is no system in place, half-inch binders for each course are the most practical for organizing content. Larger binders, in which every course is included and all homework is kept, becomes too cumbersome. With one binder for each course, the student can take one notebook and one text book to each class. This ensures that when materials are given to the student and they are then placed into the notebook on hand, that the material has a greater chance of being filed correctly.

The binders themselves should have a consistent structure, yet not be too difficult to use. For example, work that is ready to be submitted to teachers should be in the inside pocket of the binder. In this way, as soon as the student opens the binder for class, the material is right there to be turned in to the teacher. The student should divide the binder into three sections by using subject dividers. The first is current work. That includes the handouts, resources, graphs or other teacher generated materials that are current with the class content. Also in this section are current assignments that the student is in the progress of completing. This helps when work is begun outside of class, as all necessary materials are kept in one place. The second section should include student notes. This is where a few sheets of paper, not the whole ream, is kept to record lecture based information. The last section consists of material that has been covered and assessed from class. All assessments (and other graded material) are kept in this section so that the student can have a realistic picture of his or her progress in a class. The student may even have a log at the front of this section which lists grades by categories. Listing quiz, test, project and assignment grades on one sheet of paper allows for more accurate perceptions of a student's current grade.

For the student with NLD, this binder system, while simple, meets the need for external structure. The method is not overwhelming as there are only three places to put materials; however, the sections allow for greater efficiency for taking in material and for returning the work completed to the teacher. After the student becomes comfortable with the system, efforts should be made to personalize the approach to meet specific needs.

Allowing the Right Amount of Time for Service Delivery

After reviewing the intervention strategies that have been presented here, it is important to consider the quantity of time necessary to accomplish these goals within the context of the school day. The balance between maintaining a student's commitment to each class and the need to address areas of weakness is a significant challenge. Neither can be short changed.

The student with NLD has the right and need to participate in courses where he or she meet the prerequisite skills. Both to engage the student intellectually and to address issues of socialization, the student needs to be part of a diverse curriculum with age peers. In addition, the underlying skills that allow the student to be successful in the regular education setting have to be developed. One foot cannot be moved without the other.

The conversation that needs to occur with the student and the IEP team focuses on what is the appropriate amount of time in each setting. The greatest benefit for the student is to have a consistent amount of time each day with the special educator. For most students with NLD the minimum quantity would be sixty minutes each day. In order to prepare the student for any schedule changes, review the study skills system, establish academic priorities, develop skills, and address emotional needs, the special educator and the student will need at least an hour each day. This may mean that the student takes one less course; however, the benefit of skill growth and competency in each of their other courses is more important than that one additional course.

Through specialized instruction, the student with NLD can become aware of his or her academic potential. With strategies and new skills in place, the student sees that the ideas that have been circulating in his or her mind can be translated to a format that others can appreciate and teachers can evaluate. These keys for learning are what have been missing for the student for too many educational years.

In the development of written language skills, the intention of the intervention is to step back and look at the core elements of a good sentence, paragraph and essay. The special educator takes the student's creative ideas and demonstrates the formula for a written format. This modeling allows the student to see how his or her thoughts can be mapped into a coherent form. By consistently following this structure, the ideas begin to be formed within the format provided. Students then see that the distance from creative thought to written product is not as far as they had originally perceived. Having the map in front of them, allows the student to have a less burdensome journey.

Reading comprehension follows a similar route. The student is presented with an overview of the steps involved in decoding a piece of writing to encourage a better understanding of the material. The educator verbalizes those strategies that good readers all ready possess and allows the student to practice these skills with the teacher. By modeling the kinds of questions that need to be internalized and outlining a structure for note taking, the educator provides the student with the keys for cracking open a novel or text. It cannot be assumed that the student has those questions in place and knows how to use them. While other students are able to glean this didactic process of reading through participation in the classroom and their own personal reading, the student with NLD needs to have this process verbally presented to them. Their perceptions of a good reader need to accurately reflect all of the skills used to read well.

While mathematics tends to be the most challenging and frustrating of the academic areas for the student with NLD, the use of the student's verbal strengths to unlock their understanding of these concepts is the key to developing their competencies. Using student/teacher developed scripts is one strategy that relies less on math's visual cues. In addition, providing the students with organizational strategies that provide routine and structure to note taking and assignment completion is also important. Further, the student with NLD needs the appropriate textbook and other resources that match his or her learning style. When the right strategies and materials are available, the student with NLD can begin to harness mathematical concepts.

Developing a study skills system must include the student and their individualized approach to learning. The system should also not be so cumbersome that the student avoids using it when working independently in regular classes. It should also assist the student in developing an accurate assessment of their progress in a class. With the daily reinforcement of the special educator reviewing each component of the system, the approach will help the student to incorporate this process into his or her repertoire of academic skills.

While the specialized instruction needs of the student with NLD may appear extreme, having the right balance of time for one-on-one instruction and access to the regular curriculum is important. The student with NLD has a need to be with age peers to access his or her verbal skills in class discussion, gain further knowledge, and practice socialization skills. However, these students also need time with the special educator to develop skills and to interpret the general curriculum. Establishing the right balance can be challenging, but neither environment can be short changed by the other.

The strategies and practices that apply to students with NLD are based on the special educator's knowledge of the specific needs of these students. It is critical when determining the appropriate instructional program to have that information at hand. Specialized instruction is based on an understanding of a student's cognitive strengths and navigating around any processing challenges. With the right chart, academic skills can improve.

CHAPTER 12

The Nature of Accommodations

Identifying Adaptations to Student Programs

For any student who receives special education services, the IEP is the scaffolding that supports the student's educational program. It is the basis to evaluate if the school is serving the student's individual needs. The plan is divided into four definitive sections. The Present Levels section identifies the student's academic and emotional strengths and challenges. The Service Page determines the level of special education and support services that are warranted based on the student's academic profile. The Accommodations section documents the kind of adaptations that are needed to be made to the student's program so that he or she can access their education. Finally, the Individual Goal and Objectives portion of the plan outlines those areas that the student should make obtainable growth is if the appropriate academic program is in place.

It is the Accommodations section of the IEP that is most distinguishable for the student with NLD. While the other components are valuable, it is the Accommodations section that defines the student's obstacles to accessing an education. As determined by their learning style, these students require highly specific accommodations that may not be found in other Individual Education Plans. Just as the instructional strategies are strictly delineated, so are the kinds and extent of program accommodations included for students with a nonverbal learning disability.

As was stated in the previous chapter, program accommodations are very different from modifications. Accommodations are adaptations to the current curriculum and delivery of content, while modifications impact what curriculum is taught. In most cases, accommodations to the program will meet the needs of students with NLD. Varying the delivery of instruction and the forms of assessment will address the majority of their needs across academic areas.

Assessment Accommodations

When discussing the kinds of accommodations that are included for assessment purposes, it is first important to consider the purpose of any assessment. This is a tool used by educators to determine a student's competency with the material and concepts presented. The tool should not be an obstacle to determining the student's comprehension and integration of the material. In other words, the assessment used should garnish a fair measure of the student's learning and not evaluate the student's ability to maneuver through the examination.

Identifying the appropriate tool for assessment is the beginning of the process. As has been stated, students with nonverbal learning disabilities are best able to articulate their understanding of concepts verbally. Their use of language allows them to access those ideas that have been stored in their memory. Essay or short answer frameworks can best allow these students to communicate their competency with the material. In some cases, this may mean that the answers to these questions are given to the teacher individually, so that the spoken word is used. Often, just the accommodation to complete an assessment in a smaller quiet setting will meet this need. The student can then quietly read the question aloud and recite the answer before recording it on the test, or an educator may read the question and record the student's answer.

If the format of the class better follows the structure of a multiple choice or other objective form, the questions and possible answers will need to be read to the student. It will be important that the educator cue the student to stay on topic. With a variety of possible answers provided, the student's verbal strengths may trigger an overwhelming number of ideas. The accommodation then becomes that the special educator will read the question and cue key points in the assessment. This can be an appropriate student accommodation.

For longer assessments which may cover multiple themes and concepts, it will be important that the test be accommodated to group questions by topic. This is similar to the situation when multiple answers are provided. Clumping questions by theme allows students with nonverbal learning disabilities to access their verbal strengths more efficiently. When moving from topic to topic within one assessment, the test is then used to determine how well the student can shift from one idea to another. It is not evaluating a student's mastery of the material.

A student's grade on an assessment should match the teacher's knowledge of the student's competency with the material. If the student has superior grades on class work, home work and other opportunities that demonstrate a student's understanding, then the grade on the assessment should also be superior. It is when there is a disconnect between other measures of understanding and the assessment that the tool needs to be reevaluated. The teacher's understanding of a student's competencies should prevail over the grade on a single assessment tool.

Curricular Accommodations

The learning style of a student is the primary consideration when developing any accommodations. This is especially true when addressing curricular accommodations. Those changes to the materials used in the classroom and to the student expectations for learning constitute the curricular accommodations.

Textbooks, novels, computer based activities, worksheets and other support materials used to develop a student's understanding need to be considered. If given a choice of textbooks, students with NLD benefit most from written material with the least amount of visual distractions. To the extent that this challenges the student's ability to access the content, the student may require an accommodation which allows for textbook choice or that the reading material is accommodated to minimize the visual representations. This can be done by copying the pages and cutting out the pictures, graphs, etc.

Also in line with the student's learning style, the student may need an accommodation that allows for all written text to be available through audio tape or text to voice computer software. As the visual distractions of text can take away from the student's understanding, the access to auditory representations can allow the student to engage with written work at a level commensurate with his or her ability.

Another possible accommodation can focus on the use of the computer to locate information and complete classroom based assignments. The overload of visual stimuli on the computer can make locating information extremely challenging. The student with NLD may need to be provided with the specific internet location or possibly be given the information (without having to access it through the internet).

Requirements for the completion of reinforcement assignments also need to be considered regarding possible accommodations. Considering the quantity of time needed to complete a written assignment for students with NLD, the due date of the assignment, the length of the assignment, and/or the quality versus quantity of the activity may need accommodations. The dilemma with extended time for written work is that additional assignments may be given as the original work is being completed. The regular education teacher, in consultation with the special educator, may need to determine when one assignment is complete and another may begin.

In the area of mathematics, assignments may need to be chunked so that the student with NLD is allowed to demonstrate understanding of the most challenging problems rather than completing all of the assigned work. As the amount of time to process information visually is challenged, the need to complete each of the problems may need to be reduced. In addition, these students may need to have sample problems at the start of each problem set to cue the steps involved. This may also need to occur during assessments. They should also have access to calculators when their ability to complete simple functions is not being assessed. In that way, they can attend primarily to the steps of the problem and not to their fluency with math facts.

Directions on written assignments may need to be included on the list of accommodations. Reading through a long detailed description of an assignment where the directions may be imbedded can be extremely challenging for the student with NLD. The purpose of directions is to clarify the teacher's expectations, not to confuse the student. Students with NLD have difficulty identifying the key information amongst a long list of facts. Having the teacher highlight the key words or provide alternative directions that only include the primary points may need to be considered as an accommodation.

Curricular accommodations ensure that the format of the material used to reinforce a concept is not an obstacle to learning. Understanding that visual stimuli can cause confusion, addressing the time needed to process and complete written tasks and providing clear expectations are important considerations for students with NLD.

Classroom Accommodations

As was true of curricular accommodations, the student with NLD must have classroom accommodations in line with his or her individual learning style. Accessing information through the ears as opposed to the eyes is the basis for these accommodations. Teachers need to consider how material is presented and reinforced in class, how assignments are communicated, and how understanding can be verified for this student.

With regards to classroom instruction, the student with NLD must rely on auditory and language strengths to gather new knowledge. Students with NLD should have access to teacher notes so that they do not attempt to take notes while engaging with the new material. In addition, the use of questioning and classroom based discussion needs to be included to assist with further mastery of the material.

When assignments are given in class, the teacher must always provide a verbal review of the purpose and intent of the assignment. The teacher needs to clarify the expectations, the deadlines, and the format required. Allowing students, in general, to ask questions and restate the expectations enhances the learning opportunities of students with NLD.

If classroom discussion is a significant portion of the class grade, these students may need access to some questions in advance. Minimally, they should have a course outline which gives advance notice of the topics that will be covered so that they will be prepared for discussion. Further, if students are evaluated on their presentations to the class, the student with NLD may need to have the opportunity to present to the teacher alone, or with a pre-selected group of peers. The possible anxiety of disseminating information to classmates may become an obstacle and prevent the student with NLD from demonstrating an understanding of the material.

Another important consideration is that students with NLD often do not have an accurate perception of their understanding of the course content. It is not until the assessment that they are able to validate their competency with the material. The student with NLD may present to the classroom teacher that he or she is in control of the learning and engaged with the class. The assessment is a wake up call for the teacher that this student does not comprehend. One accommodation that may be included is daily verification and/or review of the day's concepts. A quick check in with the student at the end of the period to verify understanding and to review the recording of class assignments is extremely helpful and can alleviate poor assessment grades in the future.

Accommodations specific to the classroom verify the role of auditory learning and the need to validate the student's understanding. The student with NLD can present little affective behavior to indicate that he or she is struggling with the content of the class. Clear teacher expectations and discussions with the student can allow success in the classroom.

Behavior Plan

Behavior Plans can serve different roles in the Individual Education Plan. For the student with NLD, this plan can address those emotional issues that can intervene with success in the regular classroom. Often, it is the anxiety created by the social demands and varied routine of the classroom that can become an obstacle for learning. Developing a plan in advance for those behaviors can be part of the student's list of accommodations.

Discussing the options that a student has when feeling overwhelmed by the demands of the classroom is important for this student to know. Understanding that steps are in place for these occasions can be part of the student's strategy for managing feelings. This plan may include access to a safe place when the student begins to feel stress. The student is allowed to leave the classroom with limited cueing to the classroom teacher. In this way, the student does not draw undue attention. The student is then required to go directly to the location identified and to process the situation that is causing the stress. The student is not penalized for leaving the classroom, but may be asked to complete academic work from that class once emotions are in check. The student should not be allowed to avoid the academics that have occurred; however, may have an accommodated amount of work to complete.

More significant behaviors such as cutting classes, making poor social choices, and committing other non-safety school violations could be included in the list of accommodations. If these situations are a pattern of behavior that is resultant from the NLD, the team may develop a series of consequences that is outside of the school's typical list of interventions. They may include a progression of responses including increased time in the resource room, time with the teacher after school or weekends, and possibly even an in school suspension. While the actions of the student need to be outlined, it is always important to determine the underlying cause of the behaviors and to address the choices at the root cause. Assuming that students with NLD can manage their emotions in high stress situations does not consider the intense challenges that they are presented with at school.

In the case of behaviors that are considered safety violations (putting themselves or others at risk) the school administration needs to have the option for short-term removal from school. This allows the academic team the opportunity to address the emotions therapeutically and to determine if the current IEP plan is meeting the student's needs. Emotions that have stepped into the arena of personal safety need to be considered beyond their impact to the individual student and may indicate emotions that cannot be addressed in the regular education environment. These considerations could also be part of the student's list of accommodations.

Putting in place a behavior plan as part of the student's IEP forces the team to discuss possible behaviors and the team's resultant actions. When the student, parents, and educators have planned in advance of a situation, better decisions are made. This is not to say that the plan will never be adapted as different behaviors are presented and responses are developed. However, the team needs to take the time to identify potential emotional difficulties and the manner in which educators and administrators may respond.

The accommodations section of the Individual Education Plan is the road map to negotiating a specific student's learning style. It is the list of directions that educators wish all students had so that expectations are clear and obstacles to learning are articulated.

Identifying the appropriate assessment tool and determining how the assessment is given are key components to testing accommodations. Based on the team's knowledge of the student, the extent of the adaptation of the evaluative tool will be defined. Whether the kind of test is the sole accommodation or if the manner in which the test is given and how responses are recorded is also included depends upon the severity of the student's disability. What is most important is that the educator has a fair assessment of the student's ability and is not receiving a grade that is only a measure of the student's ability to complete the task.

Curricular accommodations define the materials and format that educators are to use when presenting material and determining reinforcement activities. Determining the most advantageous means for these students to access concepts and to integrate ideas with previously learned material allows them to achieve at a level commensurate with their ability. Use of verbal strengths and minimizing the use of visual cues provides students with NLD classroom assignments that allow them to succeed.

The focus on the auditory strengths of the student with nonverbal learning disabilities is also important when developing classroom accommodations. Providing these students with verbal reinforcement for all written material, whether it is a quick review of directions or detailed verification of the expectations of an assignment, addresses these students' needs for constant clarification. The use of classroom dialogue to review concepts also solidifies their understanding of the material.

While the idea of a behavior plan may have a negative connotation, in truth it provides these students with opportunities to address the emotional demands of the academic setting in a constructive way. One point on the plan may include allowing the student to access a room in the school that is less stimulating and reinforces strategies for managing stress. Another portion of the plan could include an established list of responses to choices that are not allowed under school policy. While this could be part of the accommodations list, the team should also consider the underlying issues related to these behaviors. The team must also consider potential responses to behaviors that are considered safety issues, whether for the student or for others in the school building.

With these guidelines in place, educators have the information they need to provide the kind of educational program that is both academically and emotionally appropriate. The program is clear and well articulated and is based on evaluative data and the student's previous experiences in school. When the team reviews all of its options and identifies those criterions that are appropriate to their child, the student has the greatest potential for academic success.

CHAPTER 13

Transition Planning

Identifying the Right Environment

As the student with NLD enters the first year of high school, the educational team begins thoughtful planning for the student's years after high school. As with every step in planning for their program, the careful consideration of all options and the matching of cognitive and academic strengths with program are essential. For any student entering high school, the choices appear endless and the narrowing down of possibilities is critical.

Successful transition planning infers that the student is the focus of all decisions made and that identifying the right environment is the first step. While the early years of an educational program for a student with NLD often focuses on finding the right program to meet their educational needs, as the high school years approach, the team's attention should then shift to those settings where the student is most successful. Where have the student's successes occurred? Where does the student feel most comfortable and accepted? What coursework does the student choose to work on first? Helping the student to find a niche in a school or work environment is important to limiting the number of post secondary choices the student has to make.

When looking for the right environment for success, certain characteristics specific to the student with NLD should be considered. Knowing the need for routine and structure with limited social interactions can be some of the guidelines.

Careers, such as culinary arts, sciences, or the law, allow these students to work in environments with established guidelines and factual bases. Fields which require interpretation, changing schedules and public presentations could create unnecessary anxiety for these students.

Matching the student to the right field is a drama that most parents and children work through during the high school years. Not all decisions are final, nor should they be. Most importantly, the team needs to base its decisions on the lessons that it has already learned about the abilities and needs of the child. Taking the time to list what has been learned and using that information for making decisions helps to make choices based on good information and not on assumptions.

When are They Ready for College and When are They Not

As the student and the educational team work to identify the primary interest areas, they must also consider the student's readiness for entering a post secondary program after high school. Factors to consider should include the student's understanding and acceptance of his or her educational needs. The team should also think about the student's ability to live in different environments. Is he or she ready to leave home and live independently? Further, the commitment of the student to the post secondary plan weighs into this decision of readiness.

Those students who are knowledgeable about their learning style and the systems that need to be in place for them to be successful are prepared to accept assistance from new team members. These students are aware of their cognitive abilities, know what it takes for them to be successful, and can solicit the help needed from the adults in their life. Other students with NLD who continue to misperceive their learning issues as lack of focus, see teachers as being unclear, or cannot identify the environments which create stress are still discovering what it is to be NLD. This does not mean that they have to wait for a post secondary program, but that their education may need to focus on continuing to develop this understanding and to solidify the skills and systems that they need to access their education.

Education after high school does not have to conform to the traditional model of four year liberal arts college. Post secondary plans can include hands-on vocational training, a combination of work and college coursework, or experience and training in the military. The level of structure and the need for active engagement with their area of interest may determine which of these settings is most appropriate.

One of the most significant changes in any student's move to adulthood is the change of living environment. The predictability and solitude of home is replaced by roommates, cramped quarters, and constant activity. Some students with NLD are prepared for this change, others are not. Having opportunities early on, either through overnight camps or traveling with family, may give the team the information it needs to see if the student is ready for this change. Some students may need to lengthen the transition to a post secondary program by living at home and commuting to school. This allows for one change to occur at a time: first school then the living situation. An intermediate step could be to select a college that is within an hour's distance from home so frequent visits or weekends home are possible.

One of the final considerations when determining whether the student with NLD is ready for a post secondary plan is the student's commitment to the decision. The use of a MAPS session where the student, family and friends outline the student's history, personal and professional dreams and obstacles to the dreams is helpful. The student with NLD should be given the questions in advance of a MAPS session so that he or she can consider and formulate responses. Having the opportunity to verbalize what they see as their personal and educational history and to articulate their dreams clarifies the entire team's perception of the student's future direction. It also allows the educational team to take its direction from the student and not from other invested team members. This allows the student to commit to the plan and to understand the dreams that team members have for them.

Building the Bridge to the New Setting

Once the choices have been limited, the team then begins to map how this transition will occur. Visiting the new learning environment, especially at a time when other students are present, allows the student and family to assess the kinds of resources that are available and accessible. In addition, the student will need to meet the new members of the team to begin to establish a rapport with these individuals. Finally, the student needs to develop a list of needs, those programs and systems that must be in place to encourage success.

Again, it is important that the student sees and experiences what the program will be like when students are in attendance. Summer and winter holidays, when the campus is abandoned, does not allow the student to see the true activity and intensity of some programs. It is often recommended that a visit occur in the student's junior year of high school so that more than one visit can take place prior to a decision being made.

This visit is also the time to explore how the support services work. Do they appear to work effectively and efficiently to meet a student's needs, or is the support services department overwhelmed by the demands of their students. Speaking with a student who currently accesses support services would be ideal as only those who are currently part of the system will be able to share how the system works. The site visit should also include the opportunity in sitting through a potential course, and a walk through of the student's residences.

While visiting the program, the student and family should schedule time with the student's possible new team members. This would include the coordinator of support services, the student's academic advisor, a tutor (if that fits into the student's plan), and/or other support services. In addition, meeting with a resident dean who supports students housing needs would be valuable. Again, this is the student's opportunity to begin to make connections with the receiving team. Talking through specific needs and formulating informed opinions about service providers is an important component in deciding the appropriateness of a program.

Either before the site visit or after, the student with NLD needs to develop a learning profile that can be shared with their new program staff. This is the student's own list of strengths and challenges, the environment he or she sees as necessary to learn and study, and questions that the student has about the new school. Whether this list is generated from a MAPS session or with the help of a school counselor, the student begins to act as a consumer of educational services and can then decide which program lives up to their expectations. Having clear cut criterion to evaluate a future post secondary setting allows decisions to be based on real information and not solely on personal reactions.

The Transition to Post Secondary Programs

At this point in the process, the role of the special educator takes on a new dynamic. Instead of providing the specialized instruction for the student, the teacher is now facilitating the move to the next program. The first step is determining when and how the student's confidential information is shared with the new supports. Once the release of information is given, the special educator can begin to provide the information and training that needs to occur prior to the transition. This role can take on many forms. It can include identifying resources, preparing the student for interviews, assisting in evaluating resources and support services, and meeting with service providers to share strategies and systems that have worked for the student.

Prior to the release of information by the student to the receiving program, the student and his or her parents need to decide the extent to which information is shared. While some may not choose to share that the student is receiving IEP services as they are concerned that it may impact their acceptance, there are benefits to providing the information in advance of a student's acceptance to a program. First, this allows the student access to the individuals and resources so that they can evaluate their effectiveness. In addition, the receiving school may better understand the student's transcript and possible variance of grades. Being honest with the receiving program from the start may foster a stronger relationship between educators and student.

Once the decision is made to release information and to allow communication between service providers, the special educator can assist the student in preparing for interviews and the application process. Developing a resource file which includes letters of recommendation, current transcripts, recognitions both in the school and community, application forms from schools of interest, a completed Common Application for Undergraduate College Admission which many post secondary schools require, and a senior essay that has been edited by at least one educator are key documents to consider. In addition, the student must have copies of his or her most recent comprehensive evaluation and IEP. Although not every one of these documents may be needed for the student's first post-secondary adventure, they may be needed for later adult experiences.

With documents in hand, the NLD student is prepared to provide required information to new settings. The special educator, with assistance from the school counselor, then develops a list of questions for the new program as well as a brief description of the student's personal learning style. As scripts have worked in the past to prepare the NLD student for anxiety provoking situations, this fact continues to hold true in their early adult lives. Preparing for meetings and interviews with admissions counselors and service providers begins with a general description of the process and what to expect. Possible questions that may be asked of the student should be reviewed and responses developed. Also, informed questions should be outlined by the student so they can engage the interviewer when given the opportunity. Finally, the student should have a well-articulated statement of his or her own learning style so that the kinds and extent of the supports needed can be identified.

Once the interview process has occurred and the student has identified the programs he or she wishes to pursue, the special educator can then begin to communicate with the receiving support services. If the student has adequately conveyed specific needs to the new staff, this interaction may be minimal. Primarily the special educator is making their expertise and experience available to the new educators. Allowing information and strategies to be shared can pave the way for consistent supports to be provided.

Mindful transition planning allows the student and educational team to control the process. This should begin at least two years prior to graduation so that each phase in the process has adequate time to meet the stated objective. Determining when and how information is shared, compiling the needed documents, developing scripts for interviews, and evaluating new support services takes valuable time. Each part of the decision making process ensures that the final outcome is in line with the student's needs and future goals.

Moving from IEP to 504

During the student's Annual Review of the IEP, it is important for the team to thoroughly consider the Accommodations section of the plan. When the student moves from an undergraduate program to a post-secondary phase of education, it is the Accommodations section that is most relevant. While goals and services are considerations as skills and competencies are developed, it is the Accommodations section that is considered by the new program. A thorough review should occur prior to the student's senior year so that accommodations can be considered as they would apply to a post-graduate program.

When the student graduates, services provided by the IEP are no longer available. The Accommodations outlined, however, become the 504 plan. This plan will follow them in either the academic, vocational or professional world. These are the program adaptations that allow these students access to any one of these programs. The Accommodations section of the IEP must honestly and accurately reflect the student's needs for program access.

As each accommodation is reviewed, team members should ask themselves first, if the accommodation is still necessary so that the student can access an education, and second, is it is clear enough so that a new team will understand its intent. Some accommodations may have become internalized by the student at this point in his or her education, (sitting closest to the classroom's focal point), or they no longer address the student's academic program, (access to a calculator when completing computation problems). Accommodations need to be updated each year, and this is especially true before the post-secondary transition. In addition, this list should be assessed for clarity. If the accommodation states a modification is needed for assessments or quantity of work, it should also include what that accommodation should look like. Any educator should be able to pick up this document and know what programmatic adaptations must occur for this student.

Moving from the protections of an IEP to the accommodations of a 504 plan may produce a new level of anxiety for the student and parents. Having a viable document in place prior to graduation ensures that the receiving program will have the necessary adaptations in place.

College Is Not a Simple Fix

The time from identification of a disability to the completion of the undergraduate program is a significant phase is the student's development as a learner. However, the completion of high school does not mean that the student's learning style and needs are eliminated. Instead the skills that have been developed are now tested in a new environment that will have its own set of expectations.

The first consideration is the change of environment. Moving from home with an accommodating family to a dormitory with roommates needs to be discussed prior to the move occurring. Discussions around negotiating rules for a shared space and having flexibility in expectations is very important. Sharing information with the new roommate about his or her learning style and academic needs may be an important decision to make. In addition, the student may need to investigate social opportunities that are available in the new school setting to identify safe and comfortable situations in which to develop new friendships. Again, offering possible obstacles for the first months at school and planning strategies for circumventing these is important preplanning.

Another assumption often made is that all the strategies are in place for the student, so support services are not needed. While the student may feel that the environment of their home school has been mastered, each educational setting dictates new expectations. All students, NLD or not, should be encouraged to access the resources available to them from the beginning. Assistance can always be eliminated based on successes in their new setting; however, this should not occur prior to the student's completion of the first year of the program.

The belief that change of environment will fix all challenges of the past is based more on hope then reality. Instead, the new setting is yet another opportunity for the student to develop an understanding of personal strengths and needs. Embracing their learning style not as an obstacle but as their road map to meeting their goals is more appropriate. The young adult student will make gains once he or she accepts the manner in which they learn.

Transition planning for any high school student requires reflective thought. Articulating strengths, passions, desires, and challenges is not something that most young adults feel comfortable doing. Their educational path has been dictated for many years, and while they state that they desire greater independence, the opportunity to determine their next course is very threatening.

Beginning the process early in the student's high school years ensures that the time to consider all the options is available. Creating opportunities to ponder and discuss a student's personal and academic history, needs, passions, strengths, fears, and obstacles opens the dialogue for student, parents, friends and educators. Using this information to guide the process allows the student to direct the track taken.

As the student narrows the field of choices, the investigative phase begins. With a well-developed set of questions and a detailed description of the student's learning style, the young adult and parents visit the possible choices. Seeing the new setting with other students present allows the student to begin to experience what this change will be like. There is no substitution for walking across a campus and absorbing what life is like beyond high school.

The transition bridge to the new setting is built with appropriate documents in hand and relationships fostered through good communication. The special educator plays an important role in identifying those materials that should be included in the transition file and providing information to the new service providers. Allowing the current supports to transfer history, strategies, and strengths to the new systems ensures that past lessons are incorporated into the new plan.

One document that needs specific attention in the transition process is the Accommodations section of the Individual Education Plan. A review of this section of the IEP should occur every year. However, two years prior to the completion of high school, the team should view this section with the eye of a post secondary educator. Does it have the clarity and application potential for a college or other institution? If not, corrections need to be made and revisions can be incorporated into the 504 plan that will follow them beyond high school.

The final consideration of student and parent is the realization that change of venue does not mean change of learning style. The lessons that were hard learned in the primary and secondary grades have a new setting for application.

Whether the student enters the world of work or continues in their education, the history that has all ready been created cannot be forgotten. New opportunities, in work, school or living situation, foster a greater understanding of the individual and allow for successes to occur.

CHAPTER 14

Frequently Asked Questions

What Is Section 504?

As part of the Rehabilitation Act of 1973, Congress passed Section 504, a civil rights law to protect people with disabilities by eliminating barriers and allowing full participation in areas such as education and the workplace. Since then, the Office for Civil Rights has developed federal regulations that help to explain this law.

While the law doesn't provide any new funding for programs and agencies that comply, it carries the threat of withholding federal funds from those that don't. Since public schools receive federal tax dollars, the law applies to them. It doesn't apply to many private schools because they don't receive any money from the federal government.

Who Is Eligible?

"Handicapped person" is defined by Section 504 as a person with a mental or physical impairment that limits one or more major life activities, such as caring for oneself, performing manual tasks, walking, seeing, hearing, speaking, breathing, learning, and working, to a substantial degree.

All students with Individualized Education Programs (IEP) are covered automatically under Section 504. Almost 9% of the nation's students aged 6-21 receive special education services, with a little more than half of them identified as "specific learning disability." Because necessary accommodations are included in the IEP, there's no need to write a separate Section 504 plan for these students.

Section 504 is a civil rights law to protect people with disabilities by eliminating barriers and allowing full participation in areas such as education and the workplace.

It's been estimated that 1-2 percent of students may be eligible under Section 504 alone. However, this includes students with mental, physical, and emotional disabilities, and not just learning disabilities. For example, a child with diabetes may need help from school staff to monitor blood sugar levels but have no problems with the educational program itself.

Eligibility under Section 504 isn't a consolation prize for students who aren't eligible for special education. A diagnosis of AD/HD doesn't automatically make your child eligible either. Before deciding whether she's eligible, your child is assessed by staff at the public school she attends. Then the Section 504 team considers all information about her. They must agree that she has a substantial (not mild or moderate) and pervasive (broad, comprehensive) impairment to make her eligible under this federal law.

In deciding whether a limitation is substantial, the Section 504 team also considers if your child uses a "mitigating measure"—a device or practice she uses on her own to reduce or eliminate the effects of her impairment. For example, if she tests with normal vision when wearing eyeglasses you've provided, then her visual impairment is not substantial.

If your child regularly earns report card grades of A's, B's and some C's, has standardized achievement tests scores in the average range and above, displays appropriate behavior, and attends school regularly, it 's likely that she's not substantially impaired according to this particular law. If your child has problems in only one area, such as written language or math calculation, there's a good chance that the team will find she doesn't have a disability that substantially limits her learning.

Section 504 does not require the school to maximize your child's learning. For Section 504 purposes, the school will compare your child's performance to that of the average child without disabilities.

What Is a Section 504 Plan?

If your child is eligible, then a Section 504 Plan will be developed to give her access to the general education curriculum. Unlike the IEP for special education, there are no legal requirements for what should be included in the plan. A free appropriate public education (FAPE) under Section 504 often means identifying reasonable accommodations to help her succeed in the classroom. An accommodation plan usually addresses the following:

- Nature of the disability and major life activity it limits
- Basis for determining the disability
- Educational impact of the disability
- Necessary accommodations
- Placement in the least restrictive environment (LRE)

What Are My Rights?

The law doesn't require parent participation in the meetings where a child's 504 plan is discussed. Nor does the law require parental permission to assess the child, or agree with the plan. However, many schools do include parents in the process. The law does require that schools let you know when they plan to evaluate your child or make a significant change in her educational placement.

The Section 504 Coordinator for your school or district can advise you about grievance and due process procedures if you have a disagreement. You can request a copy of the district's Section Section 504 policy, as well.

What is an IEP?

The IEP, Individualized Education Program, is a written document that's developed for each public school child who's eligible for special education. The IEP is created through a team effort and reviewed at least once a year.

Before an IEP can be written, your child must be eligible for special education. By federal law, a multidisciplinary team must determine that (1) she's a child with a disability and (2) requires special education and related services to benefit from the general education program.

The Individuals with Disabilities Education Act (IDEA), a federal law, requires certain information to be included in the IEP but doesn't specify how the IEP should look. Because states and local school systems may include additional information, forms differ from state to state and may vary between school systems within a state. You can find out about your state laws and regulations through our state level resources.

IEP Team Members

The members of the multidisciplinary team who write your child's IEP include:

- The IEP team considers the way—to the maximum extent appropriate for both—to educate your child alongside kids without a disability.
- You, the parents, who have valuable insights and information about her strengths and needs and ideas for enhancing her education.
- Regular education teacher(s) who can share information about classroom expectations and your child's performance.
- A special education teacher who has training and experience in educating children with disabilities and in working with other educators to plan accommodations.

- An individual who can interpret the results of your child's evaluation and use results to help plan an appropriate instructional program.
- A representative of the school system who knows about special education services and has the authority to commit resources.
- Individuals with knowledge or special expertise about your child that are invited by you and/or the school district.
- Representatives from transition services agencies, when such services are being discussed.
- Your child, when appropriate, and whenever transition is discussed.

Contents of the IEP

The IEP is a document that's designed to meet your child's unique educational needs. It's not a contract, but it does guarantee the necessary supports and services that are agreed upon and written in for your child.

At the least, the IEP must contain these pieces of information:

- Present Levels of Educational Performance
- Information about your child's strengths and needs is presented by teachers, parents, and the school staff who evaluated her. Comments will be made about how your child is doing in the classroom. Observations and results of state and district-wide tests and the special education assessment, including individually administered standardized tests, are reviewed. Besides academic needs, any other areas of concern that have been identified, such as language development, behavior, or social skills, should be discussed, as well.
- Goals and Objectives/Benchmarks
- The next step is to write measurable goals that she can reasonably accomplish in one year. Goals are based on what was discussed and documented in Present Levels and focus on her

needs that result from the disability. Goals should help her be involved and progress in the general curriculum and may be academic, social, behavioral, self-help, or address other educational needs. Goals are not written to maintain skills or help her achieve above grade level.

- Each goal is broken down into short-term objectives or benchmarks that provide you and the teacher ways to measure educational progress. Progress on your child's objectives/benchmarks is reported to you throughout the year—as often as the school sends out report cards.
- Special Education and Related Services
- Once the IEP is written, the team has to decide how to put it into action. The school district is obligated to provide a free appropriate public education (FAPE) in the least restrictive environment (LRE). So the IEP team considers the way to the maximum extent appropriate for both is to educate your child alongside kids without a disability. Special education is a set of services, rather than a specific place for your child to go. The services your child needs to reach the goals and objectives and how they'll be delivered are identified. For most kids, the general education classroom will be the preferred setting, but a range of options is available, including special day classes.
- In addition to the above, the following are part of the IEP:
- The extent, if any, to which your child will not participate with nondisabled kids in the regular class and other school activities.
- Whether she will take state and district-wide tests, with or without accommodations, or have an alternative assessment.
- When services will begin, where and how often they'll be provided, and how long they'll last.
- Transition service needs (age 14 or younger) or necessary transition services (age 16 or younger).
- These special factors will be considered and addressed in the IEP, depending on your child's needs:
- Supports and strategies for behavior management, if behavior interferes with her learning or the learning of others.

- Language needs as related to the IEP if she has limited mastery, or proficiency, in English.
- Communication needs.
- Assistive technology devices or services required in order to receive FAPE.
- Necessary accommodations in the general education classroom.
- Your Role at the Meeting
- Parents often feel overwhelmed when they attend an IEP meeting because so many people are there. The time goes by quickly, and you may feel rushed. Education jargon can be hard to understand, yet you're supposed to be a full participant in the meeting.
- Here are some ideas that may help to reduce your anxiety, increase your participation, and facilitate the process.
- Communicate regularly with school staff so that you'll have an idea of what the teachers may say at the meeting.
- Prepare your thoughts before the meeting by writing down the important points you want to make about your child. Download the IEP Planning Form to help you focus on major issues. If you'd like, ask to have your information included in your child's IEP.
- Expect to receive copies of reports at the meeting. If they're ready, you can ask for copies ahead of time, but be aware that many educators finish up reports the night before the meeting.
- Take someone with you to serve as your support system. If a spouse or family member can't attend, ask a trusted friend to go with you.
- Ask questions if you don't understand the terms being used. If necessary, arrange to meet with individuals after the meeting to review their statements or reports.
- Try to stay focused and positive. If anyone becomes frustrated or angry, ask to have the meeting continued at another date. It's hard to develop an IEP when emotions have taken over the process.
- Remember that you can sign to show you participated in the

meeting, but you don't have to agree to the goals or services at the meeting. You can take the IEP home to review, get input, and return later.

What Happens Next

Written parent permission is necessary before the IEP can go into effect. If you agree with only parts of the IEP, let the school know so services can begin for your child.

If you change your mind after signing the IEP, you may withdraw your permission. The best way to do that is to write a letter that tells the school why you've changed your mind and which parts of the IEP you disagree with. Most likely, the school will want to hold another IEP meeting to discuss your concerns.

The IEP is reviewed at least once a year. However, if you or the teacher believe that your child isn't learning or making progress, a meeting may be scheduled to revise the IEP. If you feel that an IEP review meeting is needed, put your request in writing and send it to the school and/or district administrator.

Work collaboratively with the staff responsible for your child's IEP. Ask what you can do to reinforce skills at home.

The questions and answers presented in this
Frequently Asked Questions
section were acquired from the website
www.SchwabLearning.org
and are the work of
JAN BAUMEL, M.S., *Licensed Educational Psychologist*

References

Forest. M. (Ed.). (1987). More education/integration. Downsview, Ontario: G. Allan Roeher Institute.

Forest, M., & Lusthaus, E. (1987). The kaleidoscope: Challenge to the cascade. In M. Forest (Ed.), More Education/Integration (pp. 1–16).

Myklebust, H. R. (1975). Nonverbal learning disabilities: Assessment and intervention. In H. R. Myklebust (Ed.), Progress in learning disabilities (Vol. 3, pp. 85–121). New York: Grune & Stratton.

Reitan, R. M., & Wolfson, D. (1993). The Halstead–Reitan neuropsychological test battery: Theory and clinical interpretation (2nd ed.). South Tucson, AZ: Neuropsychology Press.

Rourke, B. P., Young, G. C., & Flewelling, R. W. (1971). The relationships between WISC verbal-performance discrepancies and selected verbal, auditory-perceptual, visual-perceptual, and problem-solving abilities in children with learning disabilities. *Journal of Clinical Psychology, 27*, 475–479.

Rourke, B. P., Dietrich, D. M., & Young, G. C. (1973). Significance of WISC verbal-performance discrepancies for younger children with learning disabilities. *Perceptual and Motor Skills, 36*, 275–282.

Rourke, B. P., & Fisk, J. L. (1981). Socio-emotional disturbances of learning disabled children: The role of central processing deficits. *Bulletin of the Orton Society, 31*, 77-88.

Rourke, B. P. (1987). Syndrome of nonverbal learning disabilities: The final common pathway of white-matter disease/dysfunction? *The Clinical Neuropsychologist, 1*, 209–234.

Rourke, B. P. (1988). Socio-emotional disturbances of learning-disabled children. *Journal of Consulting and Clinical Psychology, 56*, 801–810.

Rourke, B. P. (1988). The syndrome of nonverbal learning disabilities: Developmental manifestations in neurological disease, disorder, and dysfunction. *The Clinical Neuropsychologist, 2*, 293–330.

Rourke, B. P. (1988). Socioemotional disturbances of learning-disabled children. *Journal of Consulting and Clinical Psychology, 56*, 801–810.

Rourke, B. P. (1989). Nonverbal learning disabilities: The syndrome and the model. New York: Guilford Press.

Rourke, B. P. (1989). Nonverbal learning disabilities, socio-emotional disturbance, and suicide: A reply to Fletcher, Kowalchuk & King, and Bigler. *Journal of Learning Disabilities*, 21, 186–187.

Rourke, B. P., DelDotto, J. E., Rourke, S. B., & Casey, J. E. (1990). Nonverbal learning disabilities: The syndrome and a case study. *Journal of School Psychology*, 28, 361–385.

Rourke, B. P. (Ed.). (1991). Neuropsychological validation of learning disability subtypes. New York: Guilford Press.

Rourke, B. P. (1991). Validation of learning disability subtypes: An overview. In B. P. Rourke (Ed.), *Neuropsychological Validation of Learning Disability Subtypes* (pp. 3–11). New York: Guilford Press.

Rourke, B. P., & Fuerst, D. R. (1991). *Learning disabilities and psychosocial functioning: A neuropsychological perspective.* New York: Guilford Press.

Rourke, B. P., & Fuerst, D. R. (1992). Psychosocial dimensions of learning disability subtypes: Neuropsychological studies in the Windsor Laboratory. *School Psychology Review*, 21, 360–373.

Rourke, B. P. (1993). Arithmetic disabilities, specific and otherwise: A neuropsychological perspective. *Journal of Learning Disabilities*, 26, 214–226.

Rourke, B. P. (1993). *Nonverbal Learning Disabilities Scale.* Windsor, Ontario: University of Windsor.

Rourke, B. P. (1995). Introduction: The NLD syndrome and the white matter model. In B. P. Rourke (Ed.), *Syndrome of nonverbal learning disabilities: Neurodevelopmental manifestations* (pp. 1–26). New York: Guilford Press.

Rourke, B. P. (1995). Treatment program for children with NLD. In B. P. Rourke (Ed.), *Syndrome of nonverbal learning disabilities: Neurodevelopmental manifestations* (pp. 497–508). New York: Guilford Press.

Rourke, B. P., & Fuerst, D. R. (1996). Psychosocial dimensions of learning disability subtypes. *Assessment*, 3, 277–290.

Rourke, B. P., & Tsatsanis, K. D. (1996). Syndrome of nonverbal learning disabilities: Psycholinguistic assets and deficits. *Topics in Language Disorders*, 16, 30–44.

Rourke, B. P., & Tsatsanis, K. D. (2000). Syndrome of nonverbal learning disabilities and asperger syndrome. In A. Klin, F. Volkmar, & S. S. Sparrow (Eds.), *Asperger Syndrome* (pp. 231–253). New York: Guilford Press.

REFERENCES

Linda J. Hudson and the Maple Leaf Center, Inc. staff are proud to host conferences around the U.S. on Nonverbal Learning Disabilities and Social Skills Training. We are your resource center for books, tapes, toys and learning aides for products relating to NLD and Social Skills Training. We are excited to offer you these products to assist you in providing your individual best whether in clinical applications, teaching, consultation, research, or parenting.

About the Syndrome of Nonverbal Learning Disabilities

Nonverbal Learning Disabilities is a specific pattern of neuropsychological assets and deficits. The 'nonverbal' of NLD does not mean that these individuals are 'not' verbal. To the contrary, they are often overly verbal, not knowing when to end a conversation. They also have a tendency to interrupt to join in on a conversation. They learn best verbally, so they hear the words but may not interpret the facial or body expressions of the person who is speaking. Therefore, understanding the true meaning of what someone is saying can be a real challenge for those with NLD. As a result, they tend to suffer socially. They can get frustrated, overwhelmed, and become withdrawn. Generally they excel in spelling and reading, but struggle with reading comprehension, math, writing, and the sciences. By teaching the individual about their strengths and weaknesses and by putting appropriate interventions in place as early as possible, individuals with NLD can succeed!

For more information about NLD, our conferences and resources, contact:

Maple Leaf Center, Inc.

President, Linda J. Hudson
www.MapleLeafCenter.com
167 North Main Street
Wallingford, VT 05773
Phone: (802) 446-3601
Fax: (802) 446-3801
Email: MapleLeaf@vermontel.net

Maple Leaf Clinic

Director, Dr. Dean J.M. Mooney
www.MapleLeafClinic.com
167 North Main Street
Wallingford, VT 05773
Phone: (802) 446-3577
Fax: (802) 446-3801
Email: MapleLeaf@vermontel.net

Book Dr. Mooney to present for your school, organization or group
NLD: From Strategies through Interventions for Home and School

Dr. Mooney's presentation will provide participants with an overview of how the syndrome of NLD can affect the student and their classroom setting. The presentation will include brain structure and functions, developmental manifestations, assessment, and will place particular emphasis on intervention/remediation techniques for both home and the classroom. A discussion of the comparison between Nonverbal Learning Disabilities and Asperger's Syndrome will take place. The role of parents, regular and special education teachers, guidance counselors, and school psychologists working with students with NLD will be explored. Case studies will be presented and a question and answer session will be included.

Schedule an Evaluation—Psychoeducational—Comprehensive Psychological—Neuropsychological
Do you need an initial diagnosis? Is it time for a current re-evaluation because it has been so long since your last evaluation? Are you not comfortable with your current diagnosis or just want to confirm that diagnosis and would like a second opinion?

Schedule a Therapy Appointment
Do you, individually or as a family, need some short-term or long-term on-going support either weekly, bi-weekly, or monthly?

Schedule a Phone or an Office Consultation
Did you just receive a diagnosis and you're asking yourself ' NOW WHAT? Do you need some help to formulate your 'action plan'? Did you form your own 'action plan' but would like to make sure that you're heading in the right direction and haven't missed something?

Camp Maple Leaf
Maple Leaf Clinic
Director, Dr. Dean J.M. Mooney
www.MapleLeafClinic.com
167 North Main Street
Wallingford, VT 05773
Phone: (802) 446-3577
Fax: (802) 446-3801
Email: MapleLeaf@vermontel.net

A fun day camp experience that focuses on _social skills and *leisure/relaxation skills* development for children and adolescents diagnosed with Nonverbal Learning Disabilities, Asperger's Syndrome, High-Functioning Autism or PDD-NOS.

Philosophy
Children with Nonverbal Learning Disabilities, Asperger's Syndrome, High Functioning Autism, or PDD-NOS need a structured and nurturing environment in order to learn, practice, and master social skills. Camp Maple Leaf offers opportunities for campers to expand their social skills while having fun, learning new leisure activities, and taking social risks. This productive and supportive environment is fostered by trained peer counselors and highly qualified staff dedicated to a kind and professional learning environment.

Goals
Campers will participate in activities that will enhance appropriate social skills; be provided with opportunities to develop friendships in a carefully structured, nurturing environment; learn skills to appropriately manage sensory issues that can transfer to the home and school environment; and have many opportunities to have fun!

Online Resources

www.MagicFoundation.org
MAGIC provides a wide array of informational, educational and support services. The Foundation's Vision is to provide a system to complete that no child has to suffer from the lack of awareness (and subsequently never treated) regarding a preventable or treatable problem. Dr. Dean Mooney presents at the Magic Foundation's annual conference in Chicago on Nonverbal Learning Disabilities and Turner Syndrome.

www.MapleLeafCenter.com
Linda J. Hudson and the Maple Leaf Center staff host conferences around the U.S. on Nonverbal Learning Disabilities and Social Skills Training. They are your resource center for books, tapes, toys and learning aides for NLD and Social Skills. They are excited to offer you these products to assist you in providing your individual best whether in clinical applications, teaching, consultation, research, or parenting.

www.MapleLeafClinic.com
Maple Leaf Clinic, founded by Dr. Dean J.M. Mooney, focuses on assessments of children, adolescents and adults (educational, psychological, neuropsychological), therapy over the lifespan, consultation (clinical and educational), supervision, and professional development. Maple Leaf Clinic is also proud to sponsor Camp Maple Leaf, a week long summer camp that caters to the social needs of campers with Nonverbal Learning Disabilities, Asperger's Syndrome, and High Functioning Autism.

www.nld-bprourke.ca
This site is designed to explain my perspectives regarding the syndrome of nonverbal learning disabilities (NLD) and related matters. I felt it necessary to do so for the following reasons: (1) I have encountered much misinformation with respect to my views about NLD. So, I decided it would be well to set the record straight; (2) I am often asked about literature regarding NLD. So, another purpose of this site is to provide references to such work; (3)There are a number of questions about NLD that are posed to me quite often. The Questions and Answers section of the site provides some responses to these queries. Hopefully, this site will expand and evolve in ways that are of interest and helpful to the concerned reader.

www.NLDontheWeb.org
Co-created by Pamela B. Tanguay, author of *Nonverbal Learning Disabilities at Home: A Parent's Guide*, and *Nonverbal Learning Disabilities At School: Educating Students with NLD, Asperger Syndrome, and Related*. Whether you are the parent of

a child with NLD, a teacher looking for information on this disorder, or a professional interested in broadening your understanding of NLD, you should visit this site.

www.Taalliance.org/centers

Parent Training and Information Centers and Community Parent Resource Centers Each state is home to at least one parent center. Parent centers serve families of children and young adults from birth to age 22 with all disabilities: physical, cognitive, emotional, and learning. They help families obtain appropriate education and services for their children with disabilities; work to improve education results for all children; train and inform parents and professionals on a variety of topics; resolve problems between families and schools or other agencies; and connect children with disabilities to community resources that address their needs.

www.Turner-Syndrome-US.org

Enabling innovations in health & learning for Turner syndrome women worldwide! The Society is a non-profit public service organization with a two-fold mission: 1) to enable innovations in health for Turner syndrome women by: a) working with health-care professionals to expand knowledge about the condition, its diagnosis, treatment, & prevention through research; and b) promoting the successful rearing, affirmation, and support of individuals affected by the condition. 2) to enable innovations in learning for Turner syndrome women by: a) providing a public forum for communication of state-of-the-art information, exchange of ideas, and social support, b) increasing public awareness of Turner syndrome, its effects, & its possibilities.

www.VCFSEF.org

Welcome to the Official Web Site of the Velo-Cardio-Facial Syndrome (VCFS) Educational Foundation, Inc. The Foundation is an international not-for-profit organization dedicated to providing support and information to individuals who are affected by Velo-Cardio-Facial syndrome, their families, physicians and other practitioners. The Foundation is independent of—and not affiliated with—any particular institution.

www.Williams-Syndrome.org

The Williams Syndrome Association is dedicated to enriching the lives of individuals with characteristics of Williams syndrome. We do this by: 1) providing information and emotional support to individuals with characteristics of Williams syndrome, their families and the professionals who work with them; 2) developing programs and services to help build strengths and meet challenges from early childhood through adulthood; 3) increasing public awareness and understanding of Williams syndrome; and 4) encouraging and supporting research into a wide range of issues related to Williams syndrome.